Welcome to
Table Talk

G000108374

Table Talk helps children and adults explore the
Bible together. Each day provides a short family
Bible time which, with your own adaptation, could work for ages 4 to 12. It includes
optional follow–on material which takes the passage further for older children. There are
also suggestions for linking **Table Talk** with **XTB** children's notes.

**Who can use
Table Talk?**

Table Talk

A short family Bible time for daily
use. Table Talk takes about five
minutes, maybe at breakfast,
or after an evening meal. Choose
whatever time and place suits you
best as a family. Table Talk includes
a simple discussion starter or
activity that leads into a short
Bible reading. This is followed
by a few questions.

- **Families**
- **One adult with one child**
- **A teenager with a younger
  brother or sister**
- **Children's leaders with their groups**
- **Any other mix that works for you!**

XTB

XTB children's notes help 7-11 year olds to get
into the Bible for themselves. They are based on
the same Bible passages as **Table Talk**.
You will find suggestions for how **XTB** can be
used alongside **Table Talk** on the next page.

In the next three pages you'll find suggestions for how to use Table Talk, along with hints
and tips for adapting it to your own situation. If you've never done anything like this
before, check out our web page for further help (go to www.thegoodbook.co.uk and click
on Daily Reading) or write in for a fact sheet.

THE SMALL PRINT

Table Talk is published by The Good Book Company, 37 Elm Road, New Malden, Surrey, KT3 3HB
Tel: 0845 225 0880. www.thegoodbook.co.uk email: alison@thegoodbook.co.uk Written by Alison Mitchell
and Mark Tomlinson. Fab pictures by Kirsty McAllister. Bible quotations taken from the Good News Bible.
AUSTRALIA: Distributed by Matthias Media. Tel: (02) 9663 1478; email: info@matthiasmedia.com.au

HOW TO USE
Table Talk

Table Talk is designed to last for up to three months. How you use it depends on what works for you. We have included 65 full days of material in this issue, plus some more low-key suggestions for another 26 days (at the back of the book). We would like to encourage you to work at establishing a pattern of family reading. The first two weeks are the hardest!

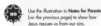
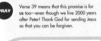

KEYPOINT
This is the main point you should be trying to convey. Don't read this out—it often gives away the end of the story!

Table Talk is based on the same Bible passages as *XTB*, but usually only asks for two or three verses to be read out loud. The full *XTB* passage is listed at the top of each **Table Talk** page. If you are using **Table Talk** with older children, read the full *XTB* passage rather than the shorter version.

The main part of **Table Talk** is designed to be suitable for younger children. *Building Up* includes more difficult questions designed for older children, or those with more Bible knowledge.

As far as possible, if your children are old enough to read the Bible verses for themselves, encourage them to find the answers in the passage and to tell you which verse the answer is in. This will help them to get used to handling the Bible for themselves.

The **Building Up** section is optional. It is designed to build on the passage studied in Table Talk (and XTB). Building Up includes some additional questions which reinforce the main teaching point, apply the teaching more directly, or follow up any difficult issues raised by the passage.

Linking with *XTB*

The **XTB** children's notes are based on the same passages as **Table Talk**. There are a number of ways in which you can link the two together:
- Children do **XTB** on their own. Parents then follow these up later (see suggestions below).
- A child and adult work through **XTB** together.
- A family uses **Table Talk** together at breakfast. Older children then use **XTB** on their own later.
- You use **Table Talk** on its own, with no link to **XTB**.

FOLLOWING UP XTB

If your child uses **XTB** on their own it can be helpful to ask them later to show you (or tell you) what they've done. Some useful starter questions are:

- Can you tell me what the reading was about?

- Is there anything you didn't understand or want to ask about?

- Did anything surprise you in the reading? Was there anything that would have surprised the people who first saw it or read about it?

- What did you learn about God, Jesus or the Holy Spirit?

- Is there anything you're going to do as a result of reading this passage?

Table Talk is deliberately not too ambitious. Most families find it quite hard to set up a regular pattern of reading the Bible together—and when they do meet, time is often short. So **Table Talk** is designed to be quick and easy to use, needing little in the way of extra materials, apart from pen and paper now and then.

BUT!!

Most families have special times when they **can** be more ambitious, or do have some extra time available. Here are some suggestions for how you can use **Table Talk** as the basis for a special family adventure...

PICNIC

Take Table Talk with you on a family picnic. Thank God for His beautiful Creation.

WALK

Go for a walk together. Stop somewhere with a good view and read Genesis 1v1—2v4.

GETTING TOGETHER

Invite another family for a meal, and to read the Bible together. The children could make a poster based on the passage.

MUSEUM

Visit a museum to see a display from Bible times. Use it to remind yourselves that the Bible tells us about real people and real history.

HOLIDAYS

Set aside a special time each day while on holiday. Choose some unusual places to read the Bible together—on the beach, up a mountain, in a boat... Take some photos to put on your Table Talk display when you get back from holiday.

You could try one of the special holiday editions of XTB and Table Talk—**Christmas Unpacked, Easter Unscrambled** and **Summer Signposts.**

Have an
adventure!

FOOD!

Eat some food linked with the passage you are studying. For example Manna (biscuits made with honey, Exodus 16v31), Unleavened bread or Honeycomb (Matthew 3v4— but don't try the locusts!)

DISPLAY AREA

We find it easier to remember and understand what we learn when we have something to look at. Make a Table Talk display area, for pictures, Bible verses and prayers. Add to it regularly.

VIDEO

A wide range of Bible videos are available—from simple cartoon stories, to whole Gospels filmed with real life actors. (Your local Christian bookshop should have a range.) Choose one that ties in with the passages you are reading together. _**Note:**_ Use the video **in addition** to the Bible passage, not **instead** of it!

PRAYER DIARY

As a special project, make a family prayer diary. Use it to keep a note of things you pray for—and the answers God gives you. This can be a tremendous help to children (and parents!) to learn to trust God in prayer as we see how He answers over time.

Go on—try it!

DRAMA OR PUPPETS

Take time to dramatise a Bible story. Maybe act it out (with costumes if possible) or make some simple puppets to retell the story.

Enough of the introduction, let's get going...

Get a jigsaw puzzle with no more than 50 pieces and do it with your child(ren), but before giving it to them remove 4/5 pieces and hide them. It will become clear to them that not all the pieces are there.

Make the point that until we can see and understand the 'Big Picture' of the Bible, it is very difficult to know what it is all about. Each individual piece of the jigsaw puzzle is like one story or book of the Bible.

Over the next 10 days we are going to see the 'Big Picture' of the Bible as we consider the huge question, 'Who will be King?'.

Who would become king or queen of the United Kingdom if the present one died? In the U.K. there are clear rules that decide who would become the next ruler. But who is king of you, and how is that decided?

These are the questions we will be answering over the next 10 days, as we follow the story of the Bible from start to finish. Throughout the following pages and in XTB too, you will see some great pictures, helping us to learn and remember what the Bible is all about. They are from a brand new booklet called, 'Who Will Be King?' It would be helpful for you and your child(ren) to have a copy.

WHO WILL BE KING?
If you would like a free copy of this booklet, please **write to:** Table Talk, The Good Book Company, 37 Elm Road, New Malden, Surrey, KT3 3HB; **or email:** alison@thegoodbook.co.uk

KEYPOINT
God made everything in the world, including us.

Today's passages are:
Table Talk: Genesis 1v1 & 31
XTB: Genesis 1v1

TABLE TALK (Optional) Quickly and secretly, each make something from play dough and hide it under a cloth. Remove the cloth and discuss which model belongs to whom.

READ **Read Genesis 1v1 & 31**

TALK What did God create? (Heavens and the earth.) Is there anything that God didn't create? What was God's creation like? (It was very good.) Who does the world and everything in it belong to? (God)

THINK Think about all that God has created and make a list of as many different things as you can. What are your favourites?

DO Create your own, 'Who will be king?' booklet, by taking a piece of A4 paper, cutting it in half, putting the two pieces together and folding them to make a booklet of eight sides. On the front cover draw a crown and write the words, 'Who will be King?' Over the next ten days we will be completing our own booklet.

PRAY Thank God for the wonderful world He has made. Ask Him to help you to learn more about the Big Picture of the Bible in the next few days.

Building up
As a family, try and find out about one other country a month, using the internet or books like 'Operation World' or 'You too can change the World' [both produced by OM (Operation Mobilisation)]. Pray for these countries and their people.

DAY 2
King of everything

KEYPOINT
God is King of everything, including us, and deserves to be treated as our King.

Today's passages are:
Table Talk: Revelation 4v11
XTB: Revelation 4v11

TABLE TALK

Choose someone and, for five minutes, treat them like the king/queen. Discuss why we treats kings/queens in a special way. Do they always deserve this?

READ

Today we go to the last book of the Bible, Revelation, to see what God deserves.
Read Revelation 4v11

TALK

To be 'worthy' means you deserve something. What does God deserve? (*Glory, honour and power.*) Why? (*He created everything.*) What does this mean He is, represented by the crown? (*King*) Who is He king over? (*Us*)

THINK

How can we show that God is King over us?

DO

On page two of your own booklet, draw the world, with some people on top. Put a large crown, labelled 'God', above them. Get your child(ren) to tell you what this means.

PRAY

Do you believe that God made everything and is the loving King of everything? If you do, thank God for helping you to believe this. Ask Him to help you obey Him as your King. If you're not sure, ask God to help you learn more about Him as you read the Bible.

Building up
If you were a king, what would you be like? Who would you be most concerned about? What new laws would you make? How do you think God is different from us?

DAY 3
Missing the mark

KEYPOINT
God has a standard and we have all failed to meet it. Our failure is because of sin.

Today's passages are:
Table Talk: Romans 3v23
XTB: Romans 3v23

TABLE TALK

Test your child with five questions about your family, including one <u>impossible</u> question. The pass mark is 5/5. Compare scores and discuss how well you did.

READ

Read Romans 3v23

TALK

What does this verse say we have fallen short of? (*The glory of God.*) This means we haven't got the pass mark God requires; we haven't met God's standard. How many people in the world have failed to reach God's pass mark or standard? A few / lots / half the world / all the world? (*All*) What word does this verse use to say what we have done wrong? (*Sin*)

What God Requires	What God Requires
Personal Score: 99%	Personal Score: 5%
God's Pass Mark: 100%	God's Pass Mark: 100%

THINK

Are you mostly good or mostly naughty? Look at the two exam papers. One person almost passed God's test and MUST have lived a good life. The other seems to have been very bad and failed badly. Which one has passed God's test? (*Neither*)

This verse in Romans tells us EVERYONE has failed to meet God's standard.

PRAY

Think of some ways that you have failed God's standard this week? (*eg: been cheeky, not been kind, told lies...*) Say sorry to God. Ask Him to help you change.

Building up
We sometimes feel bad because we often sin and let God down. Can God help us when we feel like this? **Read 1 John 1v8-9**. Try and do this every day before you go to sleep.

DAY 4
A world full of rebels

KEYPOINT
We try to be our own king instead of God. This is rebellion against Him.

Today's passages are:
Table Talk: Romans 3v10-12
XTB: Romans 3v10-12

TABLE TALK

How do you feel when you want to do something and your Dad or Mum say you can't? Do you try to do it anyway? This is called rebellion and you are a rebel.

READ

Read Romans 3v10-12

What are the three things that 'no-one' is or does in the passage? (*Righteous, understands, and seeks God*.) Righteous means 'right in God's eyes'. What has everyone done? (*Turned away*.)

TALK

King God wants us to obey Him, but we say 'No' because we want to do things our own way. We want to be king instead.

THINK

Can you think of any situation where you have disobeyed God through your words, actions or through not saying or doing something? The next picture shows us with our own crown above us and God's crown crossed out. This shows we are rebels.

Using your booklet, 'Who will be king?', turn to page three and draw the world with a big crown above it. Write God on the crown and cross the crown out. To the left of the world draw a small person with a small crown above them. Get your child to tell you what this means.

PRAY

Sin isn't just about what we do. It's also how we think. When we think it's OK for <u>us</u> to choose how to live, rather than <u>God</u> saying how to live, then we're sinning. Say sorry to God for the times when you think like that.

Building up
The Bible is a huge book, but there are some great passages to help us live God's way, with Him as our King. **Read Matthew 22v36-39**, which is known as the 'Greatest Commandment'. Think of things you can do to obey these commands.

DAY 5
Judgement day

KEYPOINT
God won't let people keep saying 'No' to Him. As the only true King, God must punish sin.

Today's passages are:
Table Talk: Hebrews 9v27-28
XTB: Hebrews 9v27

TABLE TALK

Invent a crime committed by one of you. (*eg: Dad ran down the neighbour's cat with his car.*) Discuss a range of punishments, including being let off.

READ

Read Hebrews 9v27-28

When someone breaks the law, they go to court and face an official person who does what? (*Judges them*.) When someone breaks the law it wouldn't be right to say it doesn't matter.

TALK

God won't let us keep saying 'No' to Him and pretending to be our own king. What does our passage say will happen to us? (v27) (*We will die and face God's judgement*.)

THINK

God is King of everything, even if we say 'No' to Him, and so in picture three the big crown is no longer crossed out. But the punishment for saying 'No' to God is that we are shut out of His Kingdom for ever. The picture shows this by crossing out the person instead. There must be a punishment because it wouldn't be right for God to say that sin doesn't matter.

Using your booklet, 'Who will be king?', turn to page four and draw the same picture as page three but instead of crossing out the God crown, cross out the person next to the world. Get your child(ren) to tell you what this means.

PRAY

Say sorry to God for the wrong things you do that deserve His punishment.

Building up
It's scary that our sin means we'll all be punished for ever. But read **Hebrews 9v28**. Jesus was sacrificed (died) to do what? *More about this tomorrow.*

Good news

Notes for Parents

KEYPOINT
Jesus died to take our punishment, so that we could be forgiven.

Today's passages are:
Table Talk: 1 Peter 3v18a
XTB: 1 Peter 3v18a

TABLE TALK

Recall a time when one of you was punished. What if the adult responsible had taken the punishment instead? (eg: teacher does detention, Mum misses dessert, Judge pays parking fine...) Does this ever happen?

READ

Read 1Peter 3v18a (the 'a' means just read the first sentence of this verse.)

TALK

There are so many important things for us in today's verse. Who did what, for whom and how many times? (*Jesus, died for our sins, for everyone, once.*) Jesus took our punishment.

What word tells us that Jesus was 'right with God'? (*It could be good, innocent or righteous, depending on your Bible version.*) What has Jesus' death done for us? (*Brought us to God.*)

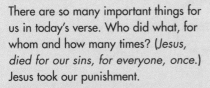

From what we have learnt so far this week, is there anything WE can do to avoid being punished? Look back to days 3 & 4 and look up Romans 3v23 & 10-12. (*No*) How should that make us feel towards both God and Jesus?

THINK

PRAY

Father God, thank you for sending Jesus to take our punishment so that we can be forgiven. Amen

Building up
Use the illustration from **Notes For Parents** to reinforce what Jesus has done for us, in setting us free from punishment.

GOOD NEWS ILLUSTRATED
The Good News for EVERYONE is that Jesus came to this earth to save the world. He lived, died, was raised to life by God and is now with His Father in heaven. The Bible calls this work of Jesus salvation.

John 3v16 is a fantastic summary verse of this fact and there are many illustrations which can help us, whether we are young or old, very intelligent or less so, to understand what Jesus has done.

Here is one, which you could use to explain and illustrate more clearly with your child(ren):

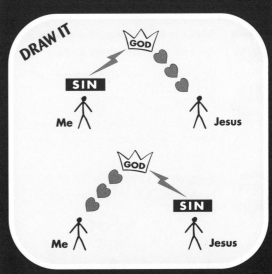

ACT IT OUT
This is us... (*hold out left hand, palm up*)... and the ceiling is God. This is our sin... (*place book on left hand*). It separates us from God, so we can't enjoy or be with Him. God must punish sin... (*thump book with fist*).

This is Jesus... (*hold out right hand, palm up*). He always perfectly obeyed God so no sin separates Him from God. But on the cross, Jesus took our sin... (*transfer book from left hand to right*).

That meant Jesus was punished by God... (*thump book with fist*). It also means that if we trust Jesus, God no longer needs to punish us, and nothing will separate us from God's love for ever... (*show free left hand*).

At the cross, God treats Jesus like us... (*right hand*), and He treats us like Jesus... (*left hand*).

DAY 7
Amazing love

TABLE TALK

Imagine or recall a situation where someone is stuck. Or, if you have a pet, put it somewhere (safe!) where it can't get out. Discuss the options. What is needed? (*A rescuer.*)

READ

Today we are looking at the greatest rescue ever. **Read John 3v16**

Who rescues who? (*God rescues us.*)

TALK

Why? (*Because He loves us so much.*)

How? (*Use the illustration in yesterday's **Notes for Parents** to help explain how God does this.*)

THINK

Everyone who trusts in Jesus can be forgiven and be with God forever. Do <u>you</u> trust Him?

DO

Using your booklet, 'Who will be king?', turn to page five and draw the world with a person standing on top, with his arms outstretched, like a cross. Draw the big God crown above and write the word 'Jesus', next to the man. Get your child(ren) to tell you what this means.

PRAY

Thank God for loving you so much that He sent His Son to die for you.

Building up
What does believing in Jesus mean? Look up **Romans 10v9-10** and see the promises written about by Paul. Believing in Jesus means <u>doing</u> what? Do you tell others about Jesus?

DAY 8
King of the world

TABLE TALK

Think of someone who has died (*pet, famous person, story character*). How does that make you feel? How did the disciples feel about Jesus' death? What was different for them?

READ

Read Acts 2v32 & 1v9-11

Who raised Jesus to life again? (*2v32 – God*) How do we know? (*2v32 – Disciples were witnesses, which means they actually saw Him.*) How do you think they would have felt after Jesus was raised to life?

TALK

I'm sure the disciples were really excited about Jesus being back with them, but did He stay with them? (*1v9 – No*) Where did He go? (*1v11 – into heaven to be with God.*) Will He stay away? (*1v11 – No, He will come back.*)

THINK

Jesus is now in heaven as King of everything. He will come back again one day. What do you think that will be like? (*Happy / sad / exciting / scary.*) Why?

DO

Using your booklet, 'Who will be king?', turn to page six and draw the world with the large 'God' crown above it. Write the word 'Jesus' on the crown too. Get your child to tell you what this means.

PRAY

Thank God for bringing Jesus back to life, and making Him the loving King of our world.

Building up
Read Ephesians 5v1-2 How should we should live, knowing that Jesus is King of everything and coming back one day?

DAY 9
A choice to make

KEYPOINT
There is a choice to be made.
There are two ways to live.

Today's passages are:
Table Talk: John 3v36
XTB: John 3v36

TABLE TALK

Play a game of choices asking the question, "would you rather... or..." Here are some examples:
• A gift or work for something
• Be taken to school in a limousine or walk alone
• Give your muddy football kit to your mum to wash, or try to do it yourself

READ

Read John 3v36

What does John say we need to do? (*Believe in the Son of God.*) This is Jesus. What is the result? (*Eternal life.*) But we have the choice to do something else. What could we do? (*Reject the Son... Jesus.*) This means saying 'No' to God and pretending to be our own king. If we do this God will shut us out of heaven for ever. We won't be with Him.

TALK

Think about the choice YOU are given by God... Believe in Jesus or keep saying 'No' to Him and live the way YOU want to. Tomorrow we will look more closely at this choice.

THINK

On page 7 of your booklet, 'Who will be king?', draw two people side by side. Under the first put an 'X' and above draw a small crown. Under the second put a tick and above draw a large God & Jesus crown. We will talk about this last picture tomorrow.

PRAY

Ask God to help you to understand and believe everything you have read today.

Building up
Read Revelation 21v22-27. This fantastic city is God's perfect kingdom and the Lamb is Jesus. Who can and can't live there for ever?

DAY 10
Two ways to live

KEYPOINT
There is a choice to be made and it comes with a cost.

Today's passages are:
Table Talk: John 3v36
XTB: John 3v36

TABLE TALK

Let's look at some more choices but this time about how we live. Do you choose:
• to only do things YOU want to do or things that others might want to do?
• to have things just for you or to share them with others?
• to be horrible or be nice to others?
Which do you choose if Jesus is your King?

READ

Read John 3v36

TALK

Look at the pictures you drew in your booklet yesterday and explain what they mean. What is the choice that needs to be made? Talk about your choice.

PRAY

IF you already know that Jesus is King of your life, then thank Him for this. Ask Him to help you keep on living for Him every day.

IF you want to start living with Jesus as your King, then pray to Him using the words printed below.

Dear God, I'm sorry that I haven't treated you as my King. I'm sorry that I've said 'No' to you by not doing what You say. Thank you that You sent Jesus to die on the cross to take away my punishment. Please forgive me, and help me to live with Jesus as my King from now on. Amen.

IF you're not sure if you want Jesus to be your King, talk about it now. And ask God to help you understand and believe what you have been learning over the last ten days.

Building up
What's next? If you choose to start living for Jesus or have done for a while:
• Talk to your family and friends about Him.
• Read your Bible regularly to learn more about living with Jesus as your King.
• Talk to God in prayer every day to ask Him to keep on forgiving you and to help you live with Jesus as your King.

Notes for Parents

The story so far from **1 Samuel**...

Chapter 1

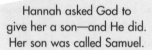

Hannah was very unhappy because she had no children.

Hannah asked God to give her a son—and He did. Her son was called Samuel.

Chapters 13 – 15

Saul <u>looked</u> great—but he wasn't! He disobeyed God's rules.

Saul turned away from God, so God took away the right of Saul's family to be kings.

Chapters 2 – 7

Samuel grew up in God's temple. He loved and served God all his life.

Samuel became the last of a group of leaders called <u>Judges</u>.

Chapter 16

God chose a new king, instead of Saul. He would be king when Saul died.

The new king was called David.

Chapter 8

When Samuel was an old man, the Israelites asked for a king to lead them.

But the Israelites already had a king! <u>God</u> was their real King.

Chapter 16v7

David was a young shepherd when God chose him. He didn't <u>look</u> much like a king!.

But God knew what David's heart was like. God knew David loved and trusted Him.

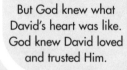

'Man looks at the outward appearance, but God looks at the heart.' 1 Samuel 16v7

Chapters 9 – 12

God chose Saul to be the first king of Israel.

Saul was very tall, very handsome, and a good soldier. He <u>looked</u> like a great king!

Chapter 17

The Israelites were at war. Their enemies had a HUGE champion called Goliath.

Saul and his soldiers were all too scared to fight Goliath. But David wasn't. He knew God would help him to win...

DAY 11
The real King

KEYPOINT
David loved and trusted God. He knew that God is the real King.

Today's passages are:
Table Talk: 1 Samuel 17v45-50
XTB: 1 Samuel 17v45-50

TABLE TALK

For the next 20 days we'll be finding out about King David from the book of **2 Samuel**. But first, check out the story so far from **1 Samuel**, in **Notes for Parents** opposite.

READ

Goliath was HUGE. But David knew that <u>God</u> is far, far greater than any man. Read what David said to Goliath in **1 Samuel 17v45-50**.

TALK

What weapons did Goliath fight with? (v45) (*Sword, spear and javelin.*) What weapon did David have? (v49) (*Sling and stones.*) But <u>who's</u> name was David fighting in? (v45) (*The name of the Lord Almighty.*) David trusted God to help him win. Was he right? (v50) (*Yes!*)

THINK

David knew that God would rescue him from Goliath. That would show the 'whole world' something very important. What was it? (v46) (*'That there is a God in Israel.'*) God is the **Real King**. He's far greater than even the tallest man, or most powerful king or president!

PRAY

Ask God to help you to learn more about Him as you read 2 Samuel. Ask Him to help you trust Him as much as David did.

Building up
Read about how God chose David to be the next king in **1 Samuel 16v1-13**. Verse 7 says that God chose by looking at the heart. What does today's story tell you about David's heart? (*He trusted God; he loved God and wanted everyone to know about Him.*)

DAY 12
Waiting for God

KEYPOINT
David knew that God would choose the right time for Saul to die. So he chose to wait.

Today's passages are:
Table Talk: 1 Samuel 26v7-12
XTB: 1 Samuel 26v7-12

TABLE TALK

What is the name of the Queen of England? (*Queen Elizabeth the Second*) Who will be the next King or Queen after her? (*Prince Charles*)

It's common for a king's son to become king after his father. BUT Saul had turned away from God. So God took away the right of Saul's family to be kings. Who had God chosen to be the next king after Saul? (*David*) How do you think Saul felt about David? (*Angry, jealous.*) Saul was so jealous of David that he kept trying to kill him! David had to run away from Saul's palace.

READ

One day, Saul took an army of 3000 men to search for David. At night, Saul slept on the ground in the middle of his army. There were thousands of soldiers around Saul, but even so David and one of his men (called Abishai) crept right up to where Saul was sleeping...
Read 1 Samuel 26v7-12

TALK

David and Abishai were right next to Saul. They could easily kill him! So why didn't they? Find two reasons in v9&10. (*v9—God had chosen Saul as king, so no-one had the right to kill him; v10—David knew that God would decide the right time for Saul to die.*)

PRAY

David chose to <u>wait</u>. He knew God would do the right thing at the right time. God's ways are <u>always</u> best. Ask Him to help you trust Him—even when that means waiting a while.

Building up
David had spared Saul's life once before. Read about it in **1 Samuel 24v1-22**.

DAY 13
A messy start

KEYPOINT
David mourned for Saul. He was upset that God's chosen king was dead.

Today's passages are:
Table Talk: 2 Samuel 1v1-4 & 11-12
XTB: 2 Samuel 1v1-16

TABLE TALK

<u>Either</u>: Give everyone one minute to find things that bring us messages (eg: letters, phone, computer...) <u>Or</u>: discuss different ways that you hear important news.

READ

2 Samuel starts with a man with torn clothes and dirt on his head! He had an important message for David...
Read 2 Samuel 1v1-4

TALK

Where had the messenger come from? (v3) (*The Israelite camp—where the army were.*) What was his message? (v4) (*Many had died in battle, including Saul and his son Jonathan.*)

READ

How do you think David felt now that Saul was dead? Talk about your ideas, then find out in **2 Samuel 1v11-12**.

What did David and his men do? (v11) (*Tore their clothes.*) Do you know why? (*It was a sign that you were very sad or upset. People in Bible times did this when they heard terrible news.*)

THINK

Saul had tried to kill David many times. So why was David sad when he heard of Saul's death? (*David knew God had chosen Saul to be king. He was upset that God's chosen king was dead.*)

PRAY

This seems a sad start to 2 Samuel, but notice that <u>God's plans</u> are working out. The day was coming when David would be king, just as God promised. Thank God that His plans <u>always</u> work out.

Building up
Read the messenger's full report in **v5-10**, then compare it with 1 Samuel 31v4. Maybe the messenger thought David would reward him for saying he'd killed Saul. But he was wrong! See 2 Samuel 1v14-16.

DAY 14
Sad song

KEYPOINT
It's sad when someone we love dies. But if you're a Christian, death will never separate you from Jesus.

Today's passages are:
Table Talk: 2 Samuel 1v23-27
XTB: 2 Samuel 1v17-27

TABLE TALK

Have a competition to see who can look **a**—happiest; **b**—most surprised; **c**—most puzzled; **d**—angriest; **e**—saddest.

READ

David was really upset about the deaths of Saul and his son Jonathan. How did he show his sadness? (*He tore his clothes.*) David also wrote a **lament**, which is a poem or song about your sadness. Read part of David's lament in **2 Samuel 1v23-27**.

TALK

Saul and Jonathan were both brave soldiers. David describes them as <u>swifter</u> than what? (v23) (*Eagles*) And <u>stronger</u> than what? (v23) (*Lions*) David was very upset (grieved) for Jonathan. Why? (v26) (*Jonathan was very dear to him.*) Jonathan had been David's best friend. He had even protected David from his father, Saul!

THINK

It's very sad when someone you love dies. God hates death too and the worst thing is that death can separate us from Him for ever. That's why God sent Jesus. Jesus can make death harmless for His followers.

PRAY

If <u>you</u> are a follower of Jesus then even death will never separate you from the love of your best friend, Jesus! Thank Him for this.

Building up
Check out **Romans 8v35-39** to see a l-o-n-g list of things that <u>can't</u> separate you from Jesus' love!

DAY 15
King at last

KEYPOINT
God kept His promise to make David king. God <u>always</u> keeps His promises.

Today's passages are:
Table Talk: 2 Samuel 2v4 & 5v1-5
XTB: 2 Samuel 2v4 & 5v1-5

TABLE TALK

Mime different 'pouring' actions for your child to guess eg: pour milk on cereals then eat them, pour milk in tea then stir it, watering a garden... Lastly mime pouring oil on someone's head! In Bible times this was how someone was made king. They were 'anointed' by having oil poured on their head.

READ

Now that Saul was dead, it was time for God's promise to David to come true. But it didn't happen all at once...
Read 2 Samuel 2v4a (The 'a' means just read the first part of the verse.)

TALK

Where was David anointed as king of? (*Judah*) Israel was divided into 12 family groups called **tribes**. David was now king of the tribe of <u>Judah</u>. Seven years later, David became king of the rest of the Israelites. **Read 2 Samuel 5v1-5**

How old was David when he became king? (v4) (*30*) How long did he rule as king? (v4) (*40 years*)

PRAY

God had first chosen David to be king when he was only a teenager. It didn't happen straight away, but God **kept** His promise. God's words <u>always</u> come true. Think about some promises of God that haven't happened yet. Ask God to help you wait and trust Him.

Building up
In **5v2**, what had the Israelites remembered? (*That God had said David would be king.*) This promise is in 1 Samuel 16v12. Can you think of other promises that God has made and kept?

DAY 16
The promise keeper

KEYPOINT
800 years before David, God promised to give His people the land of the Jebusites. He did!

Today's passages are:
Table Talk: 2 Samuel 5v6-10
XTB: 2 Samuel 5v6-16

TABLE TALK

What's the first book in the Bible? (*Genesis*) Flick back to **Genesis 15v18-21** to find a promise God made to Abraham 800 years before David was born. Who's last in the list? (*Jebusites*)

READ

800 years later, David was king over Abraham's family (the Israelites). The time had come for God to keep His promise about the land of the Jebusites...
Read 2 Samuel 5v6-10

TALK

The Jebusites laughed at David. Who did they say could keep him out? (v6) (*The blind and the lame.*) Were they right? (v7) (*No*) David and his men captured Jerusalem from the Jebusites (possibly by climbing up a water tunnel under the city). How did David become so powerful? (v10) (*God was with him.*) Jerusalem became the royal city. David built a palace there, for him and his family to live in. (v11-16)

PRAY

God kept the promise He had made to Abraham 800 years earlier. God <u>always</u> keeps His promises. Neither 800 years nor strong enemies can stop Him! Thank God that nothing (and no-one) can stop His words coming true.

Building up
Another ancient promise which God kept was His promise to send Jesus, the King of Kings who came from David's family line. **Read Luke 1v26-38**. V37 says that 'nothing is impossible with God'. Learn this together as a memory verse.

DAY 17
Promises, promises

Today's passages are:
Table Talk: 2 Samuel 5v17-25
XTB: 2 Samuel 5v17-25

TABLE TALK

Check out another of God's promises in **2 Samuel 3v18**. Who did God say David would defeat? (*The Philistines.*)

READ

Let's see how God does it...
Read 2 Samuel 5v17-21

TALK

Who did David ask before he attacked the Philistines? (v19) (*The Lord*) What did God tell David? (v19) (*'I will give you victory.'*) Did David win the battle? (v20) (*Yes*)

READ

But the Philistines came back again...
Read 2 Samuel 5v22-25

TALK

What did God tell David this time? (v23) (*Circle around behind them first, then attack.*) What was David to listen for? (v24) (*The sound of marching in the trees.*) Did David win? (v25) (*Yes*)

THINK

God showed David what to do each time, so that His promise about the Philistines came true. God shows us what to do too! How? (*In the Bible.*)

PRAY

Ask God to help you to trust Him and obey Him as David did.

Building up
Before fighting the Philistines, David asked God what to do. That's a top tip for us, too. If you're not sure about something, **ask God** to show you what to do. Talk about any situations where you aren't sure what to do. Then pray about them together.

DAY 18
Respect!

Today's passages are:
Table Talk: 2 Samuel 6v3-7
XTB: 2 Samuel 6v1-11

TABLE TALK

Play **hangman** to guess the words 'The Ark of the Covenant'. Ask your child if they know anything about the ark. Talk about their ideas, then read the info box in **Notes for Parents**.

READ

God had helped David and the Israelites capture Jerusalem. It was now the royal city, so David wanted to bring the ark into Jerusalem. **Read 2 Samuel 6v3-7**

TALK

The ark was meant to be carried on its poles, but how did David's men carry it? (v3) (*On a cart.*) Who touched the ark? (v6) (*Uzzah*) Uzzah broke God's rules. What happened to him? (v7) (*He died.*)

THINK

Does that seem too hard? If so, remember that the ark was a sign of our great, powerful God. He didn't want anyone to be killed. That's why His rule warned them not to touch the ark. But God must be treated with **respect**. His rules should never be ignored.

PRAY

In the past few days we've seen that God's words always come true. Today we've learnt that God is also powerful and dangerous. He's dangerous for those who don't listen to Him or obey Him. But (as we'll see tomorrow) He's fantastic if we listen and obey Him. Ask God to help you do that, especially when you don't want to.

Building up
Read 2 Samuel 6v8-11. How did David feel? (*v8—angry; v9—afraid.*) What did God do while the ark was with Obed-Edom? (v11) (*Blessed/was very kind to him.*) More about that tomorrow...

THE ARK OF THE COVENANT (THE COVENANT BOX)

The ark was a wooden box, covered in gold. It was carried on two wooden poles, also covered in gold. Inside the ark were two stone tablets with the Ten Commandments written on them. The ark reminded the Israelites that **God was with them**.

God had given clear rules about moving the ark. It was to be covered by the priests, then carried on its poles (Numbers 4v15). And no one was to <u>touch</u> the ark, or they would be killed.

What God is like

The Old Testament is great for showing us what God is like! Look at what we've learnt so far:

Day 11: God is the Real King

Day 13: God's plans always work out

Day 15: God's words always come true

Day 16: Nothing and no-one can stop God's plans

Day 17: God shows us how to live, in the Bible

Day 18: God must be treated with respect

As you keep reading the Bible, you'll see more of what God is like (like adding pieces to a jigsaw puzzle). Ask God to help you get to know Him better and better as you read His Word, the Bible.

KEYPOINT
David and the Israelites celebrated because they knew that God was with them.

Today's passages are:
Table Talk: 2 Samuel 6v12-15
XTB: 2 Samuel 6v12-15

TABLE TALK

<u>Recap yesterday's story:</u> What was David bringing to Jerusalem? (*The ark.*) What rules had God made about the ark? (*No one must touch it.*) What happened when Uzzah broke God's rule? (*He died.*)

READ

When Uzzah was killed for touching the ark, David was <u>scared</u>. He left the ark with a man called Obed-Edom. While it was there, God was very <u>kind</u> to Obed-Edom. **Read 2 Samuel 6v12-15**

TALK

Why was Obed-Edom being **blessed** (given good things)? (v12) (*Because he was looking after the ark.*) When David realised this, he went to bring the ark to Jerusalem. David made sacrifices (gifts) to God. Then what did David and the people do? (v14) (*He danced for God; they shouted and played trumpets.*)

THINK

David and the Israelites realised that having God with them wasn't just a <u>scary</u> thing. It was also a <u>brilliant</u> thing, worth celebrating!

PRAY

The ark reminded the Israelites that **God was with them**. If you are a Christian (a follower of Jesus) then God is with **you** all the time. How will you celebrate that God is with you? You could sing a song for Him, play a happy tune on an instrument, or even dance like David! Choose a way to celebrate, and do it now!

Building up
Read **Psalm 150** out loud to praise God together.

DAY 20
Window watching

KEYPOINT
Michal was disgusted by David's dancing, but David was dancing for <u>God</u>.

Today's passages are:
Table Talk: 2 Samuel 6v16 & 20-23
XTB: 2 Samuel 6v16-23

TABLE TALK

Some churches organise a 'walk of witness' when the people all walk through their town singing hymns. Imagine taking part and being seen by friends from school or someone you work with. What might <u>they</u> think? How would <u>you</u> feel?

READ

David was dancing in front of the ark as it came into Jerusalem. After the ark was put in a special tent, David made sacrifices (gifts) to God. Then he gave gifts of food to everyone in the crowd.
Read 2 Samuel 6v16 & 20-23

TALK

Michal was Saul's daughter and David's wife. Where did she watch David from? (v16) (*A window.*) What did she think when she saw David dancing? (v16&20) (*She was disgusted by his dancing.*) Michal thought that David was making a fool of himself in front of the people. But what did David say? (v21) (*'I will celebrate before the Lord.'*) He wasn't dancing for the people. He was dancing for <u>God</u>!

PRAY

Does worrying about what other people think ever stop you from praising or serving God? **Ask God** to help you to put Him first, and not worry what other people think.

Building up
Think of other examples when living for God might mean being laughed at by others. For example, if people at school or work are telling rude jokes and you refuse to join in. Pray about anything you are worried about, and ask God to help you to live for Him in those situations.

DAY 21
Amazing grace

KEYPOINT
David wanted to build a temple for God, but instead God promised great things for David.

Today's passages are:
Table Talk: 2 Samuel 7v1-3 & 8-11
XTB: 2 Samuel 7v1-11

TABLE TALK

How many different kinds of homes can you think of? *eg: house, flat, caravan, igloo, houseboat, palace...* Who would live in each one?

READ

King David now lived in a <u>palace</u> built of beautiful cedar wood. But the ark of God sat in a <u>tent</u>! That bothered David. It didn't seem right...
Read 2 Samuel 7v1-3

TALK

Nathan was a **prophet** (one of God's messengers). What did he tell David? (v3) (*Do whatever you have in mind.*)

READ

But that night God gave Nathan a message for David. God <u>didn't</u> want David to build Him a temple. That would be someone else's job. Instead, God made amazing **promises** to David.
Read 2 Samuel 8v8-11 and listen out for three promises...

TALK

What were the promises? (*v9—I will make your name great; v10—I will provide a place for my people to settle; v11—I will give you rest from your enemies.*)

PRAY

Wow! David had wanted to do something for God, but instead God promised to do great things for David! Think of some of the great things God has done for <u>you</u>. Thank God for His huge kindness to you.

Building up
What things can the word **grace** mean? What is <u>God's</u> grace? (*Grace is God's HUGE kindness to people who don't deserve it.*) What's the greatest example of God's grace to us? (*Sending Jesus to take the punishment we deserve.*) Thank God for this.

DAY 22 Indestructible promise

Today's passages are:
Table Talk: 2 Samuel 7v12-16
XTB: 2 Samuel 7v12-17

TABLE TALK

Think of one promise you can each make and keep today. *eg: child promising to wash up after dinner, dad promising to read to toddler before bedtime...*

READ

God had already made some great promises to David. But He wasn't finished yet! **Read 2 Samuel 7v12-16**

TALK

There are some tricky terms in these verses. These questions should help to explain them: **1**—who will become king after David's death? (v12) (*One of David's sons [offspring].*) **2**—David had wanted to build a temple for God. Who would build it instead? (v13) (*His son.*) **3**—How long would David's family serve God as kings? (v13) (*For ever!*)

THINK

When **we** make promises they're often just for a <u>short</u> time (like the ones you made earlier) or we <u>don't</u> keep them. But God's promises aren't like that! God's promise to David lasted for ever! (*We'll find out more about this promise tomorrow...*)

PRAY

Thank God that <u>nothing</u> can stop His amazing promises coming true.

Building up

Read v14-15 again. When Saul had rejected God, the Lord rejected Saul as king (1 Sam 15v26) and took His Holy Spirit away from Saul (1 Sam 16v14). God promised not to treat David's son this way. Just like a human father, God would punish the king when he did wrong. But God would always love him.

DAY 23 Christmas is coming

Today's passages are:
Table Talk: Luke 1v30-33
XTB: Luke 1v30-33

DO

Play some Christmas music, or sing a carol together. As you do, ask your child to try and work out how Christmas links with yesterday's story about God's promises to David.

READ

Let's jump to the New Testament to see God's promise coming true. We're going to listen in on an angel who has a message for a young woman called Mary... **Read Luke 1v30-33**

TALK

What was Mary's son called? (v31) (*Jesus*) Which king does the angel talk about in v32? (*David*) How long would Jesus' kingdom last? (v33) (*Forever.*)

God had promised David that someone from his family line would be king for ever. <u>Who</u> was God talking about? (*Jesus*)

THINK

Can you think of a Christmas carol with David in the title? (*Once in royal David's city.*) What does that mean? (*Jesus was born in Bethlehem, David's home town.*)

God kept His promise to David by sending Jesus. **He** is the King who will rule for ever. Is He <u>your</u> King?

PRAY

(*We'll find out more about King Jesus when we start reading John on Day 31.*) **Thank God for sending Jesus**.

Building up

Joseph (who married Mary) was also from David's family line. Read what an angel said to Joseph in **Matthew 1v18-25**.

DAY 24
David's prayer

TABLE TALK

Imagine some fabulous promises. *eg:
going to Disneyland, having your own
pony, never going to work again!* How
would feel if these were promised to you?

READ

God had made some <u>amazing</u> promises
to David. We're going to listen in as
David talks to God about how he feels...
Read 2 Samuel 7v18-22

TALK

What does David call God four or five
times in these verses? (*Sovereign Lord*).
Sovereign means God is <u>in control</u> of
everything. He is the **Real King**. What
does David tell God? (v22) (*How great
He is. That there's no-one like God.*)

DO

Write **Sovereign LORD** in the middle of
some paper. Now add some other words
that describe God. *eg: great, loving,
promise keeper...*

THINK

We've seen how great <u>God</u> is. Now look
at **v18** again. Did David think <u>he</u> was
someone great who deserved God's
goodness? (*No!*) But God was **so good**
to David. That's God's **grace**. (Grace is
God's HUGE kindness to people who
don't deserve it.) Add **grace** to your list.

PRAY

Use the words in your list in a thank you
prayer to God.

Building up
Copy out **v22**. Learn it as a memory verse.

DAY 25
Victory parade

TABLE TALK

What heading does your Bible have at
the beginning of chapter 8? (*eg: 'David's
victories'*) Chapter 8 lists David's victories
over a whole bunch of enemies. We're
not going to read <u>how</u> he won these
battles, but we are going to read <u>why</u>.
The answer is in verses 6 and 14. Listen
out for the **same words** in both verses.

READ

Read 2 Samuel 8v6 and v14

Which words were the same? (*'The LORD
gave David victory wherever he went.'*)
<u>Who</u> gave David all these victories?
(*God*)

THINK

Why do you think God gave David all
these victories? Talk about your answers,
then check back to **2 Samuel 7v11**.
(*God was keeping His promise to give
David rest from all his enemies.*)

God is the **Promise Maker** and
Promise Keeper. We can <u>always</u> trust
Him to do what He says.

DO

(*Optional*) Copy Psalm 145v13 onto
some paper: **'The Lord is faithful to
all His promises.'**
Put it where you will
see it every day.

PRAY

Talk about God being the Promise Maker
and Promise Keeper. How does that make
you feel? Pray together about it.

Building up
Read the promises in **Notes for
Parents** opposite. Turn each one into a
thank you prayer.

DAY 25
Notes for Parents

THE PROMISE MAKER

'The Lord is faithful to all His promises.' Psalm 145v13

'For God loved the world so much that He gave His only Son, so that everyone who believes in Him may not die but have eternal life.' *John 3v16*

'Everyone who calls on the name of the Lord will be saved.' *Romans 10v13*

God has said, 'Never will I leave you; never will I forsake you.' *Hebrews 13v5*

'This Jesus, who was taken from you into heaven, will come back in the same way that you saw Him go to heaven.' *Acts 1v11*

'God will not let you be tempted beyond what you can bear. But when you are tempted, He will also provide a way out so that you can stand up under it.' *1 Corinthians 10v13*

'And we know that in all things God works for the good of those who love Him, who have been called according to His purpose.' *Romans 8v28*

And remember that God promises judgement too...
'I will punish the world for its evil, the wicked for their sins.' *Isaiah 13v11*

DAY 26
What kind of king?

KEYPOINT
David gave all the treasure he had won to God. David was just and fair to his people.

Today's passages are:
Table Talk: 2 Samuel 8v7-11
XTB: 2 Samuel 8v7-18

TABLE TALK

Recap: What did we learn yesterday about <u>God</u>? (*He kept His promise to give David rest from his enemies. God is the Promise Maker and Promise Keeper.*)

READ

Today we're going to find out what chapter 8 tells us about <u>David</u>. As you read the verses, make a list of all the things David collected from his enemies. **Read 2 Samuel 8v7-10**

TALK

What do you think David did with all that treasure? Talk about your ideas, then **read verse 11** to find out.

David **dedicated** the treasure, which means he gave it to God. It was probably kept to be used for God's temple.

THINK

David gives us a good pattern to follow. Unlike David, you probably don't have much treasure! But what can <u>you</u> give to God? Talk about ways that you can give God your *time*, or the *things you are good at*, or your *money* or...

PRAY

Ask God to help you give these things to Him.

Building Up
Think of some words to describe David, beginning with **J** or **F**. (*Jolly and freckled*? *Juggling and fat*?)
Read 2 Samuel 8v15. What kind of king was David? (*Just and fair.*)
David was just and fair, doing what was right for his people. He was a <u>good</u> king. But this doesn't mean that David was **perfect**! There is only <u>one</u> perfect King in the world. Who? (*King Jesus*)

DAY 27
Mephibo-who?

KEYPOINT
David showed great kindness to Mephibosheth because of his promise to Jonathan.

Today's passages are:
Table Talk: 2 Samuel 9v1-7
XTB: 2 Samuel 9v1-13

TABLE TALK

Write MEPHIBOSHETH on some paper. In <u>one</u> minute, see how many words you can make using the letters in Mephibosheth. (*1-4: Good try; 5-9: Well done; 10-14: Fantastic!; 15+: Superstars!!!*)

READ

David had been friends with Saul's son Jonathan. So David wanted to show kindness to anyone from Saul's family...
Read 2 Samuel 9v1-7

TALK

What was Jonathan's son called? (v6) (*Mephibosheth*) What was wrong with him? (v3) (*He was lame.*) What did David promise to do for Mephibosheth? (v7) (*Show him kindness; give him the land that belonged to Saul; let him eat at the royal table.*)

THINK

Mephibosheth was part of <u>Saul's</u> family. In those days kings would murder everyone from the previous king's family, in case they tried to become king themselves. But David <u>didn't</u> do that. Why? (*See v1, and compare with 1 Samuel 20v14-15.*)

PRAY

David had <u>promised</u> not to harm any of Jonathan's family. But David did <u>much</u> more than that. He also showed **great kindness** to Mephibosheth. Tomorrow we'll see how David was behaving like God (who also shows huge kindness). Can <u>you</u> be like that too? **Who** do you know who could do with some kindness? Talk about what you can do for them, then ask God to help you to do it.

Building up
Find out how Mephibosheth became crippled in **2 Samuel 4v4**.

DAY 28
A pattern for us

KEYPOINT
David's kindness to Mephibosheth is like a picture of God's HUGE kindness to us.

Today's passages are:
Table Talk: Romans 5v10
XTB: Romans 5v10

TABLE TALK

Play 'mirrors': Stand or sit facing a partner. As you move (eg: to scratch your nose!) they have to copy what you do exactly, as if they are your reflection in a mirror. Try for a while, then swap over.

THINK

King David is like a <u>pattern</u> for us. He is God's chosen King, ruling over God's people (the Israelites) in the land God has promised to give them. So what **David** does is sometimes a picture of what **God** does. (He <u>reflects</u> what God is like.)

READ

Yesterday we saw David showing **great kindness** to an enemy. (Mephibosheth came from Saul's family, so he would be seen as David's enemy.) Mephibosheth did nothing to deserve David's kindness. David was kind because of his faithful love for Jonathan. **God** is like that too!
Read Romans 5v10

TALK

What does this verse say we used to be? (*God's enemies.*) How have we been brought back (reconciled) to God? (*By the death of God's Son, Jesus.*) Wow! We were God's enemies because of our <u>sin</u>. But God's Son, Jesus, died to take the punishment we deserve, so that we can be forgiven and brought back to God.

PRAY

David's kindness to Mephibosheth was like a picture (or reflection) of God's HUGE kindness to us. Thank God for His great kindness in sending Jesus.

Building up
Do you still have the 'Who will be King?' booklet you made on Days 1-10? If so, go through it to remind you of God's kindness in sending Jesus.

DAY 29
A close shave

KEYPOINT
David showed kindness to Hanun, but Hanun insulted God's people (and God Himself) in reply.

Today's passages are:
Table Talk: 2 Samuel 10v1-5
XTB: 2 Samuel 10v1-5

TABLE TALK

<u>Recap:</u> Who did David show kindness to? (*Mephibosheth*) What is that a picture of? (*God's huge kindness to us.*)

READ

David showed kindness to people from other countries as well. When **King Nahash** (king of the Ammonites) died, David showed kindness to his <u>son</u>...
Read 2 Samuel 10v1-5

TALK

What was the new Ammonite king called? (v1) (*Hanun*) How did David show kindness to Hanun? (v2) (*He sent men with a kind message.*) But Hanun didn't trust David! What did he do to David's men? (v4) (*Shaved half their beards and cut their clothes so their bottoms were showing!!!*)

This looks funny, but it was a terrible insult. And by insulting <u>God's people</u>, Hanun was insulting <u>God</u> too! Tomorrow we'll see what David did about it.

PRAY

Think back to Day 27. Who did you decide to show kindness to? Have you done it yet? <u>If you have</u>—great! Now think of someone else you can show kindness to. <u>If you haven't</u>, try your very best to do it today. Ask God to help you.

Building up
Read a New Testament view of showing kindness in **1 Thessalonians 5v15**. Who should we be kind to? (*'Each other' probably means other Christians; 'everyone else' means everyone else! In other words, there's no one we shouldn't be kind to!*) Who do you find it <u>hard</u> to be kind to? Pray about any difficult relationships, and ask God to help you to be kind rather than 'pay back wrong for wrong'.

DAY 30
God's ways are best

KEYPOINT
God always does what's right for His people.

Today's passages are:
Table Talk: 2 Samuel 10v9-14
XTB: 2 Samuel 10v6-19

TABLE TALK

Recap: David had wanted to show kindness to Hanun. But what did Hanun do to David's men? (*Sent them back with their beards half shaved off and their bottoms showing.*)

READ

Hanun had insulted God's people and insulted God. That meant war! Hanun's people (the Ammonites) hired lots of extra soldiers (Arameans, also called Syrians) to help them fight. The Israelite army was led by Joab and his brother Abishai...
Read 2 Samuel 10v9-14

TALK

Joab divided his army in two to fight the Ammonites and Arameans. What did the Arameans (Syrians) do? (v13) (*They fled/ran away.*) What did the Ammonites do? (v14) (*They fled.*)

Wow! The Arameans and Ammonites all ran away! In v15-19 we see that David then won a battle against the Arameans, and that loads of kings became David's servants.

<u>Before</u> the battle, Joab didn't know if he'd win or not. What did he say? (v12) (*'The LORD will do what's good in His sight.'*)

PRAY

Things may not work out for us. And God may answer our prayers differently from how we expect. But **God always does what's right for His people!** <u>Thank</u> Him for this—and <u>trust</u> Him!

Building up
Think over the story so far from **2 Samuel**. What have you learnt about <u>David</u>? And about <u>God</u>? *We'll come back to the story of King David on Day 50.*

DAYS 31-50
Notes for Parents

LET'S JOIN JOHN

Welcome to John's Gospel. The word **'Gospel'** means **'good news'**. John is telling us the good news about <u>Jesus</u>.

Before we dive into John's book, try out this quick quiz, to see how much you all know about John:

QUICK QUIZ

Are these facts **True** or **False**?

A John was one of Jesus' closest friends (called disciples). **T / F**

B John was the disciple Jesus hated. **T / F**

C John was known as 'the disciple Jesus loved'. **T / F**

D John was a famous basketball player. **T / F**

E His brother James was also a disciple. **T / F**

F John's parents were Zebedee and Salome. **T / F**

G His parents were Zebra and Salami. **T / F**

H John also wrote four other Bible books—Revelation, 1 John, 2 John and 3 John. **T / F**

Answers: Facts A, C, E, F and H are all true.

DAY 31
Believe it or not

> **KEYPOINT**
> John wrote his book to show us that Jesus is the Christ, the Son of God.

Today's passages are:
Table Talk: John 20v30-31
XTB: John 20v31

TABLE TALK

Start by reading **Notes for Parents** opposite and trying the **Quick Quiz** together.

READ

John spent a lot of time with Jesus, so he was a great person to write a book about Jesus. John even told us <u>why</u> he wrote his book... **Read John 20v30-31**

TALK

What are the <u>two</u> reasons John gives for writing his book? (v31) (*1—so we may believe in Jesus; 2—so that by believing we may have everlasting life with God.*)

THINK

What <u>two</u> titles does John give Jesus? (v31) (*Christ or Messiah, and Son of God.*) **Christ** is a Greek word, **Messiah** is Hebrew. They both mean 'the anointed one'. On Day 15 we saw that David was anointed with oil. What did that mean for David? (*It made him king.*)

The same is true for **Jesus**. Christ and Messiah mean '**God's chosen King**'. John wrote his book to show teach us that Jesus is the King who God promised would rescue His people.

PRAY

Ask God to help you to understand John's book as you read it. Ask Him to help you believe Jesus is the Christ and God's Son.

Building up

In v30, John says that he <u>didn't</u> write down all of Jesus' miracles. Talk about why that might be, and then look up part of John's reason in **John 21v25**.

DAY 32 The word on the street

Today's passages are:
Table Talk: John 1v1-4
XTB: John 1v1-4

TABLE TALK

In one minute, how many things can you think of that begin with 'W'?

READ

John's book is all about **Jesus**, but it starts by giving Jesus a title that begins with 'W'. Listen out for it as you read today's verses. **Read John 1v1-4**

What does John call Jesus? (*The Word.*)

DO

Read verses 1 and 2 again, but this time replace 'the Word' by saying 'Jesus' instead.

TALK

What does v1 tell you about <u>who</u> Jesus is? (*Jesus is God.*) How long has Jesus been around? (v2) (*He has always been around from the very beginning.*) What does v3 tell us about Jesus? (*He created everything.*) Wow! Think back to your list of 'W' words. Which ones did Jesus create? (*eg: water, our world, wind, whales, worms...*)

THINK

Which two words beginning with 'L' does John use in v4? (*Life and light.*) John mentions **life** and **light** loads in his book. He wants us to understand that trusting <u>Jesus</u> is the only way to **life** with God in heaven. *We'll read more about Jesus being our **light** tomorrow.*

PRAY

Is anyone more amazing than Jesus??? And <u>we</u> can know <u>Him</u>! Get excited and thank God.

Building up
The beginning of John sounds like the beginning of another book. Do you know which one? (*Genesis*) **Read Genesis 1v1-3**. How is it like John 1? John is saying that even before God chose to create the world, 'the Word' existed. Wow!

DAY 33 Light and wrong

Today's passages are:
Table Talk: John 1v5-9
XTB: John 1v5-9

TABLE TALK

If possible make the room very dark (or squash into a cupboard!). What it's like being in the dark? Then turn on a torch or light a candle. What difference does light make?

READ

Jesus is like a **light** to people. He shows us the truth about ourselves. He helps us to see the sin in our lives. And He shows us the way to God. **Read John 1v5-9**

TALK

Who else did God send into the world? (v6) (*John*) This <u>isn't</u> the same John whose book we're reading. This is John the Baptist. Do you know why he's called that? (*He baptised people in the Jordan river, which means he dunked them under the water! We'll read more about that on Day 36.*) What did John the Baptist come to do? (v7) (*To tell people about the light: Jesus.*)

PRAY

People who don't know Jesus are like people living in complete darkness. They need Jesus (the light) to help them see how they should live. Do <u>you</u> know anyone who doesn't know Jesus? Pray for them now. Ask God to send someone to tell them about Jesus. (It might be <u>you</u>!).

Building up
In John's book there are seven sayings, often called the 'I am' sayings. Read what Jesus says about being 'light' in **John 8v12**.

Our Family

FAMILIES ARE GREAT

For better or for worse, we are all born into families. The family is part of God's good gift to us; as the Anglican marriage service says: *'the union of husband and wife in heart, body, and mind is intended by God for their mutual joy; for the help and comfort given one another in prosperity and adversity; and, when it is God's will, for the procreation of children and their nurture in the knowledge and love of the Lord.'*

And whatever our experience of family life, everybody knows that families are a good thing. It is part of how we are made, because God is ultimately revealed in the Bible as a Family. God the Father has lived for all eternity in a relationship of love with His Son, Jesus. And as humans are made in the image of God, so we are created to be like God in this respect. We all **long** to **belong** to a loving family. And families work best when they are built around the character of God our Father.

What the Bible teaches us about families is that God made them to reflect His own character of strong, nurturing love, which is about giving, rather than getting. They are places where gifts are developed, characters formed, skills learned and maturity encouraged in a context of secure, stable love.

FAMILIES ARE FALLEN

Of course this ideal picture of family relationships has been destroyed by the Fall. Part of the curse that came on Adam and Eve as a result of their rejection of God's rule over them was that, although they would still desire true family life, their ability to achieve it would be diminished. So that families, which should be places of mutual support and love of parents and children, become places where there is a power struggle. (Genesis 3v16). Any parent knows the reality of that with a troublesome toddler, or a feisty teenager. Far more disastrous for the whole family, is when

there is a struggle for dominance between husband and wife.

Although the Bible contains examples of families which live up to these ideals, it is equally frank in exposing the disasters that result from our fallen selfishness and greed. David and Bathsheba in this issue of *Table Talk* is one example, but you can see how sin spoils the families of many of the great Bible characters: think of Joseph and his jealous brothers; or Noah and his disgrace after the flood; or Abraham's cowardice over his wife; or the squabbling of Jacob and Esau egged on by the manipulative Rebekah.

The fact of our fallenness, presumably, is why family life is defined more carefully as God gives the law to Israel. The roles and responsibilities of fathers and children are painted out in detail in Leviticus and elsewhere. And the way that adultery is considered so important as to warrant the death penalty is not just because it strikes at the very heart of the family, but also because it is such a denial of God's character—who is <u>faithful</u> above all things. Many of these principles are picked up and endorsed in the New Testament also.

And what we see in the Scriptures is played out in our daily lives. There are many family units where all is not well: an absent or domineering father; a selfish and controlling mother; a lack of care; or a casual attitude towards the spiritual life of the family.

Some people say that we should not promote the notion of God as Father, because there are those who have had such a bad experience of their fathers that the category is unhelpful for them. But the truth is that fatherhood is not an earthly category that we have applied to God. It is God's character that is given to us—and is sadly perverted in some cases. And even if people have had a bad experience of their own fathers—they still know what a real father should be like. They still long for a strong, dedicated, loving heavenly Father who will nurture them, forgive them, give them security and help them to grow.

And even if you are part of a family which, for whatever reason, is a long way from 'the ideal', you are in no way disqualified from belonging. You may be a single-parent family, or married to someone who is unbelieving, or have a cupboard full of family skeletons (not literally we hope!). But none of these sad realities of our fallen lives puts us beyond hope as far as God is concerned, because His family love and liberating forgiveness reaches out to all of us...

GOD'S GREATER FAMILY

Perhaps the most exciting thing about God's character as a family is His desire to see His family grow. The gospel is the story of how God went through immense pain and personal loss in order to build for Himself an enormous and diverse worldwide family of human children whom He adopts as His own. And by choosing to live in each new child by His Holy Spirit, He enables us to start living life as it was meant to be.

The gospel, then, can start to address many of the unhelpful patterns that we can fall into with our families. By making us part of His bigger, worldwide family, God tears down the walls that we tend to build around our lives. He makes families outward looking and inclusive of others, rather than inward looking and excluding to others.

We need to teach our children (and ourselves!) from an early age that we are part of God's great big family that stretches all around the world, and forward and backwards in time. It may be fun to start referring to others with familial names—just to make the point. Referring to brothers and sisters at church, or 'Uncle' Martin Luther, or 'Auntie' Gladys Aylward, can give children a great sense of excitement and connection with the church of the past and present.

FAMILIES ARE EVANGELISTIC

Our homes then, should be places of welcome and hospitality, rather than an exclusion zone for others. This inevitably brings with it dilemmas of various kinds. Many people practice a studied kind of hospitality, where the house is clean, the food is intricately prepared, and the children are on best behaviour. And this is right for special occasions. But we also need to learn not to be too house proud or fussy about how we present ourselves to visitors—that is what being part of a family is all about: reality, honesty and openness with others who are part of 'our family in Jesus'.

For what most people crave in hospitality, is not a shiny, cultured version, but the kick-your-shoes-off, drink tea and chat at the kitchen table, freewheeling experience of being part of the normal life of a family of fellow believers. When others are asked to participate in family life, not to sit and observe a pink-scrubbed caricature from a distance, we will discover more genuine love and a greater experience of what we are looking forward to in heaven.

There will be many Christians in your own congregation who will be delighted to be drawn into your family life in this way: single people, the elderly and younger people also. But pursuing this model of Godly family life can have an enormous evangelistic impact too. As a young man from a broken non-Christian home, I received this kind of welcome from several Christian families, and the experience was painful for me—because it made me realise what was lacking in my own upbringing. But it also made me yearn for the same thing. It taught me that belonging to God's family was the most wonderful thing imaginable, and that I was truly blessed to become a member. It is this experience of matter-of-fact inclusion and acceptance that many, many people hunger and thirst for, and it is a wonderful gift you can give to others.

Tim Thornborough

> **By making us part of His bigger, worldwide family, God tears down the walls that we tend to build around our lives. He makes families outward looking and inclusive of others, rather than inward looking and excluding to others.**

DAY 34
God's children

KEYPOINT
Everyone who trusts Jesus to rescue them from sins becomes one of God's children.

Today's passages are:
Table Talk: John 1v10-13
XTB: John 1v10-13

TABLE TALK

Recap: What has John told us about Jesus so far? (eg: Jesus is 'the Word', He is God, Jesus created everything, Jesus has always been around, Jesus is 'light'.)

READ

Wow! Jesus is amazing! So what do you think people did when Jesus came into the world—welcomed Him or refused to welcome Him? **Read John 1v10-11** to find out.

TALK

Did people welcome Jesus? (*No!*) Even many of God's special people, called Jews, refused to believe Jesus was God or that He'd come as their Rescuer (v11).

READ

But it's not all bad news...
Read John 1v12-13

What is the great news for anyone who does believe that Jesus came to rescue them? (v12) (*They become God's children.*)

THINK

How cool is that??? Everyone who trusts Jesus to rescue them from sins becomes one of God's children! If you're a Christian, then God is your Father. He looks after you, cares for you and loves you! *We'll find out more about how Jesus rescues us as we read more of John's book.*

PRAY

If you are one of God's children, thank Him now! If you're not sure, ask Him to help you find out more as you read John.

Building up
Jot down some words to describe a perfect dad. Now think about how **God** fits each of those words.

DAY 35
Jesus is God!

KEYPOINT
Jesus lived on earth as a human, and was full of grace and truth.

Today's passages are:
Table Talk: John 1v14
XTB: John 1v14-18

TABLE TALK

On five small pieces of paper write the letters **A**, **C**, **E**, **G** & **R**. Spend a minute seeing how many words you can spell with these letters: *eg: car, cage, ear, race...*

READ

Today's verse tells us more about **Jesus**. As you read it, listen out for another word that you can spell with your letters. **Read John 1v14**

TALK

What was the word you can spell with your letters? (*Grace*) What is grace? (*Grace is God's huge kindness to people who don't deserve it.*)

Verse 14 is about 'the Word'. Who is that? (*Jesus*) What did Jesus do? (*He became a human being [flesh] and lived among us.*) Jesus is **God**—but He came down from heaven to live on earth as a human.

What did the people see? (*His glory.*) They saw the amazing miracles Jesus did, things only **God** could do.

What was Jesus full of? (*Grace and truth.*) How did Jesus show His grace to us? (*He became a human and died on the cross to take the punishment for our sins, so that anyone who trusts Jesus can become one of God's children.*)

THINK

PRAY

Jesus loves us so much that He lived on earth as a human, and even died for us! That's far more than we deserve! Spend time thanking Jesus for His *grace*.

Building up
Read Philippians 2v6-8. Jesus is equal with God because He is God. But what did He do? Can you explain why? How can we be like Him (v5)?

DAY 36
It's all about Jesus

KEYPOINT
John the Baptist was the 'voice' Isaiah wrote about. He came to tell people to get ready for Jesus.

Today's passages are:
Table Talk: John 1v19-28
XTB: John 1v19-28

TABLE TALK
Play hangman to guess the word **Christ**. Ask your child if they can remember what 'Christ' means. (*'the anointed one' /God's chosen King*, see Day 31.)

READ
When John the Baptist came, baptising and teaching people, many of them wondered if he was the promised Christ (Messiah). **Read John 1v19-28** to see how John answered them.

TALK
Was John the **Christ/Messiah**? (v20) (*No*) Was he the prophet **Elijah**? (v21) (*No*) Was he the **Prophet** mentioned in Deuteronomy? (v21) (*No*) Was he the **voice** that Isaiah had talked about? (v23) (*Yes*) 700 years earlier, a man called Isaiah had said that someone would come to tell people to get ready for Jesus the Rescuer. That person was John the Baptist!

John's job was to get people ready for Jesus. What did he tell them about Jesus in v27? (*Jesus is coming after John, but is far greater than John.*)

THINK
John didn't want to be the centre of attention. He wanted everyone to know about **Jesus**, not himself. Do *you* seek attention and popularity? Or do you want Jesus to get the attention instead, so that people are talking about Him?

PRAY
Ask God to help you to be less self-centred. Ask Him to help you tell people about Jesus, like John did.

Building up
Read Isaiah's words about John the Baptist in **Isaiah 40v3-5**.

DAY 37
The lamb of God

KEYPOINT
Jesus is the lamb of God. He died as a sacrifice, to take the punishment for our sins.

Today's passages are:
Table Talk: John 1v29
XTB: John 1v29

TABLE TALK
If you could be any animal, what would you be and why?

READ
John the Baptist was doing his job of telling people about Jesus. He said that Jesus was like an animal...
Read John 1v29

TALK
Which animal did John say Jesus was like? (*A lamb.*) In Bible times, a lamb was killed and offered to God as a **sacrifice**. If someone had sinned against God, they would say sorry to Him and then offer Him a gift (sacrifice), such as a lamb.

THINK
Can you think how **Jesus** was like a lamb? (*He was killed as a sacrifice to God.*) What was the result of Jesus' death? (v29) (*It took away the sin of the world.*) When Jesus died on the cross, He took the punishment <u>we</u> deserve for all our sin. If we trust Him to, Jesus takes away all the sins we've ever done! So that we can be forgiven, and can be friends with God.

Think about wrong things you have done. (Try to be honest with each other!)

PRAY
Now thank God that Jesus can take those wrong things away and that you can forget about them.

Building up
The book of Revelation describes Jesus as 'the Lamb who was slain'. Join in with the praise, (and enjoy the picture language!), as you read **Revelation 5v1-14**.

DAY 38
Notes for Parents

TALKING ABOUT BAPTISM

For young children, it probably won't be appropriate to get involved with discussions about the purpose of baptism. Keep it simple, and just ensure they understand what John actually did (especially if they have only seen babies 'sprinkled'). The picture below will help them see that John completely submerged people in a river. (He dunked them!)

With older children, talk about what baptism is a sign of, as explained below...

Inside Outside

Is baptism the same as having a bath? Why / why not?

Being **baptised** is like being washed clean on the <u>outside</u>. Being **forgiven** is like being washed clean on the <u>inside</u>. Baptism is an outside sign of an inside change.

John could only wash people clean on the <u>outside</u> —like giving them a bath. Only **one** person can make us clean on the <u>inside</u>. Who?

WHY WAS JESUS BAPTISED?

The people who came to John to be baptised admitted that they were sinful and needed to be forgiven. John baptised **sinners** who **repented** (turned away from their sins).

But **Jesus** was very different. He lived a **perfect** life. He <u>never</u> sinned, and had no need to repent. Jesus was baptised to **please** God. It was all part of God's plan for Him.

Note: *Even John found it hard to understand why Jesus was baptised. John knew that he was the sinful one, not Jesus! Read their conversation in* **Matthew 3v13-15** *Jesus' answer shows that being baptised was part of God's plan for Him. He obeyed His Father.*

DAY 38
That's the Spirit!

KEYPOINT
John baptised with water, but only <u>Jesus</u> can make us clean inside.

Today's passages are:
Table Talk: John 1v30-34
XTB: John 1v30-34

TABLE TALK — Talk about any experience of **baptism** your child has had or seen. If they have been baptised themselves, talk about what happened. If you're waiting until they are older, talk about why.

READ — Yesterday we saw that John the Baptist called Jesus the 'Lamb of God'. Read what else John said in **John 1v30-34**.

TALK — What did John do? (v31) (*He baptised people with water.*) That means he dunked people in the river!

THINK — People got baptised by John to show they wanted to be forgiven and cleaned from sin. <u>Water</u> couldn't clean them. But <u>Jesus</u> could—by dying, like a lamb, to take their punishment.

What amazing thing did John see happen to Jesus? (v32) (*The Holy Spirit came down to Jesus like a dove.*) We know from the other Gospels that this happened when Jesus was baptised by John (eg: Mark 1v9-11).

DO — <u>Draw</u> the Spirit (as a dove) in the picture.

God gave His Spirit to Jesus to show that Jesus really was His Son. The amazing truth is that Jesus gives His Holy Spirit to <u>everyone</u> who becomes a Christian! The Holy Spirit helps Christians live for God.

PRAY — Thank God for giving the Holy Spirit to all Christians. Ask God to help you live more for Him and less for yourself.

Building up
Jesus didn't need to be baptised because He never sinned. So why was He baptised? Read about it in **Notes for Parents**.

DAY 39
Excited about Jesus

KEYPOINT
When Andrew met Jesus, he told his brother Peter all about Him. We should do the same.

Today's passages are:
Table Talk: John 1v35-42
XTB: John 1v35-42

TABLE TALK

Who are your favourite football team or sports star? In one sentence explain why you think they are great.

READ

Football fans gets really excited about their team. They talk about them all the time! In today's verses we meet someone who was really excited about <u>Jesus</u>...
Read John 1v35-39

TALK

These two men were disciples of John the Baptist. 'Disciple' means 'pupil', so these two were <u>learning</u> from John about God. What did they do when John told them that Jesus was the Lamb of God? (*They followed Jesus, called Him 'Teacher' and spent the day with Him.*)

READ

One of those two was called Andrew. He was the brother of Simon Peter (often just called Peter). **Read John 1v40-42**

When Andrew realised who Jesus was, what was the <u>first thing</u> he did? (v41) (*Told his brother about Jesus.*) Then what did Andrew do? (v42) (*Brought Simon Peter to Jesus.*)

THINK

How can <u>you</u> be like Andrew? Who will you tell about Jesus this week?

PRAY

Dear God, help us to get excited about Jesus. Please give us the courage to tell our friends and family all about Him.

Building up
These men left their homes to follow Jesus. Do <u>we</u> have to leave our homes to follow Jesus? (*No!*) What do you think it means to be a follower of Jesus today? If you're not sure, who could help you to find out?

DAY 40
Follow the leader

KEYPOINT
Philip and Nathanael became followers of Jesus too. They found He knew all about them.

Today's passages are:
Table Talk: John 1v43-50
XTB: John 1v43-50

TABLE TALK

Play a quick game of 'Follow the Leader', where one of you is the leader and the others follow your actions exactly.

READ

Yesterday we saw Andrew and Simon Peter become Jesus' first disciples. Today we'll meet two more.
Read John 1v43-46

TALK

What did Jesus say to Philip? (v43) (*Follow me/Come with me.*) Who did Philip tell about Jesus? (v45) (*Nathanael*) What was Nathanael's reaction? (v46) (*'Can anything good come from Nazareth?'*) When Nathanael met Jesus he found out the answer...

READ

Read John 1v47-50

What did Jesus know about Nathanael? (*He was a true Israelite; he'd been under the fig tree.*) Who did Nathanael say Jesus was? (v49) (*The Son of God and King of Israel.*)

THINK

Jesus knew all about Nathanael, even things that seemed impossible to know. And Jesus knows all about **you** too! What you look like, what you do, what you think. How does that make you feel?

PRAY

Thank Jesus that He knows all about you. Ask Him to help you to follow Him, especially when you find it hard.

Building up
What exactly does God know about us? Look up **Psalm 139v1-16**. How many things can you find in the psalm that God knows about us?

DAY 41
Stairway to heaven

DAY 41 & 43
Notes for Parents

KEYPOINT
Jesus is the only way to God and life with Him in heaven. (Like a staircase to heaven).

Today's passages are:
Table Talk: John 1v51
XTB: John 1v51

TABLE TALK

If you have stairs, sit on them to do today's Table Talk!

READ

Who are the four men who have become Jesus' disciples? (*Andrew, Peter, Philip, Nathanael.*) Jesus told them they would see amazing things...
Read John 1v51

TALK

What would the disciples see? (*Heaven open, and angels travelling up and down on the Son of Man.*) The **Son of Man** is a title for <u>Jesus</u>. But how could angels use Jesus like a staircase???

Read about Jacob's dream of a stairway in **Notes for Parents** opposite.

THINK

Can you think how Jesus is like a stairway to heaven?

When Jesus died and came back to life, He became the ***link*** between God and humans. Like a staircase leading up to heaven. By trusting in Jesus we can get to know God! Jesus is the <u>only</u> way to God and life with Him in heaven.

PRAY

Thank God that He wants you to know Him, and one day live with Him. Thank Him for sending Jesus to make that possible.

Building up
Read about Jaccob's dream in **Genesis 28v10-19**.

JACOB'S DREAM [DAY 41]
The book of Genesis tells us about a dream that Jacob had. In it he saw a huge stairway going from heaven to earth. Angels were travelling up and down on it. The stairway linked Jacob to God. God promised to always be with Jacob. [Genesis 28v12-15]

BUILDING UP [DAY 43]
Read **John 2v17** again and then read **Psalm 69v9**.

This psalm was written by King David. But it's also about <u>Jesus</u>! It says that Jesus is devoted to His Father's house (the temple). When the disciples saw what Jesus did in the temple, they remembered David's psalm. (*That's what John 2v17 means.*)

DAY 42
Wine sign

KEYPOINT
When Jesus performed His first miracle, His disciples believed in Him.

Today's passages are:
Table Talk: John 2v1-11
XTB: John 2v1-11

TABLE TALK

Talk about signposts. (Can you see any through the window?) What kinds of signposts can you think of? (*Road names, warnings, school signs...*) Why do we have signs?

READ

At the end of John's book he tells us that Jesus' **miracles** are like **signposts**. They point to who Jesus is, so that we can believe in Him and live with Him for ever in heaven (John 20v31). Today's story is about Jesus' *first miracle*.
Read John 2v1-11

DO

(*Optional*) Ask your children to act being the servants as you read the story again.

TALK

What did the servants put into the jars? (v7) (*Water*) What was the water changed into? (v9) (*Wine*) Who changed the water into wine? (*Jesus*) What did the disciples do? (v11) (*Believed in Jesus.*)

THINK

The disciples didn't understand everything about who Jesus was—but they DID believe in Him and followed Him. What do **you** believe about Jesus? What difference does this make to what you do?

PRAY

Ask God to help you understand more about Jesus, and believe what you read about Him in the Bible.

Building up
Read verse 4 again. John often mentions Jesus' 'time' in his book. What do you think it means? (*The time when Jesus would rescue His people by dying for them on the cross.*)

DAY 43
Temple trouble

KEYPOINT
Jesus was rightly angry that His Father's temple was being used as a market place.

Today's passages are:
Table Talk: John 2v13-17
XTB: John 2v12-17

TABLE TALK

What time of year is it? (*Autumn, Winter, Spring, Summer*) What's the next festival that's coming up? (*eg: Harvest, Christmas...*) How will you celebrate?

READ

In today's story it's **Passover** time—a time to remember how God rescued His people when they were slaves in Egypt. So we'd expect God's temple to be full of excited people, getting ready to celebrate Passover. But instead, the temple was full of greedy people, using it like a market place! Let's find out what Jesus thought about that... **Read John 2v13-17**

TALK

What did Jesus call the temple? (v16) (*'My Father's house'*) Why? (*Jesus is God's Son, so it's His Father's temple.*) Jesus was rightly angry that His Father's temple was being used as a market place. What did He do? (*See v15.*) The people who came to the temple to pray were being **cheated** out of their money. So Jesus stopped the salesmen!

PRAY

Sometimes we see things happening that we know are wrong. Talk about some examples. (*eg: if you see someone being bullied...*) If you see something like that, ask God to help you to act in the way He wants, even when that's difficult or could make you unpopular.

Building up
See **Notes for Parents** on the previous page for today's **Building Up** suggestions.

DAY 44
Temple rebuilder

Today's passages are:
Table Talk: John 2v18-22
XTB: John 2v18-25

TABLE TALK

Imagine if someone came into your classroom or workplace and started throwing the tables about! How would you feel? How about your teacher/boss?

READ

Jesus had been tipping over tables in the temple. Let's see what the Jewish leaders thought about that...
Read John 2v18-22

TALK

The Jewish leaders wanted proof that Jesus had the right to clear out the temple. What did they demand? (v18) (*A miracle as a sign.*) How did Jesus reply? (v19) (*'Destroy this temple, and I will raise it again in three days.'*) Jesus was standing in the Jewish temple when He said this. But what 'temple' was He really speaking about? (v21) (*His body.*)

THINK

What do you think He meant? (*Jesus was talking about Himself. He was going to die, but three days later God would bring Him back to life. This showed Jesus was God's Son. He had the right to clear out the temple.*)

PRAY

Jesus did have the right to clear out the temple. What rights does Jesus have over your lives? (*eg: to say 'Follow me' as He did to His first disciples.*) Pray together about your answers.

Building up
Read John 2v23-25. What did people do when they saw Jesus' miracles? (v23) (*Believed in Him.*) But their faith wasn't going to last. Many of Jesus' followers gave up on Him later on—see **John 6v66**. Jesus knew this. He knows exactly what everyone is like (v25). It's great that you're reading the Bible to get to know Jesus better. But sadly, some people give up following Jesus later. If you really want to follow Jesus, ask Him to help you never to give up.

DAY 45
Born again

Today's passages are:
Table Talk: John 3v1-8
XTB: John 3v1-8

TABLE TALK

Talk about how babies are born. (*If you're a mum, you could talk about your memories of your child being born.*) Today's story is about being born—again!

READ

In today's story we meet a Pharisee, one of the Jewish leaders. His name was Nicodemus. **Read John 3v1-8**

TALK

What did Nicodemus know about Jesus? (v2) (*Jesus had come from God.*) What did Jesus tell Nicodemus he needed to do? (v3) (*Be born again.*) But what did Nicodemus say? (v4) (*You can't go back inside your mum to be born again!*) But Jesus meant a different kind of birth. How did He say we have to be born? (v5) (*'of water and the Spirit'*). [See **Building Up** if you want to investigate this further.]

Read verse 8 again. We can't see the wind. So how do we know it's there? (*We see what it does on a windy day.*) We can't see the **Holy Spirit** either, but we can see the huge effect the Spirit has on people's lives.

PRAY

Everyone needs to be **born again**. We need to be washed clean from our wrongs, and to start again with God's Spirit helping us to live for God. If you're a Christian, then you've been 'born again'. Thank God for His Spirit. Ask Him to help you to live for Him every day.

Building up
In the Old T, God promises to sprinkle clean water on His people to clean them from their wrongs, and to give them His Spirit. **Read Ezekiel 36v25-27.** Nicodemus was a teacher of the Old T, so he should have known this!

DAY 46
Lifted up

KEYPOINT
Jesus would be 'lifted up' on the cross. Anyone who trusts in Him will have eternal life.

Today's passages are:
Table Talk: John 3v9-15
XTB: John 3v9-15

TABLE TALK

Play a quick game of **'I Spy'**.

In 'I Spy' you are an **eye-witness** of the things you see. <u>Jesus</u> was an eye-witness too... **Read John 3v9-13**

TALK

What name did Jesus give Himself? (v13) (*The Son of Man*) This title is used in the Old T about the Christ (Messiah). Jesus often used this title when talking about Himself. Where had Jesus come from? (v13) (*Heaven*) Jesus came from heaven, so He was the <u>best</u> person to teach Nicodemus (and us!) about heavenly things (v11). Jesus was an **eye-witness**.

READ

Read John 3v14-15

What did Moses lift up? (v14) (*A snake.*) In the Old T, Moses made a bronze snake. God said that anyone who looked at it would be cured from deadly snakebites.

THINK

Who else would be 'lifted up'? (v14) (*The Son of Man ie: Jesus.*) Jesus was going to be 'lifted up' too—when He was dying on the cross. And anyone who trusts in Jesus, won't just be saved from a snakebite! What will they have? (v15) (*Eternal life.*)

PRAY

The only way to live with God for ever in heaven is by believing in Jesus. Tomorrow we'll see exactly how Jesus made that possible. For now, thank God for His Son Jesus, who came from heaven to save us.

Building up
Read about Moses and the bronze snake in **Numbers 21v4-9**. Were the Israelites saved because the snake had special powers? (*No!*) Read God's words in **v8** again. Why were the people saved? (*Because they <u>trusted</u> what God said, and turned to the rescue He provided.*)

DAY 47 The most famous verse

KEYPOINT
God loves us so much that He sent His Son Jesus to die for us.

Today's passages are:
Table Talk: John 3v16
XTB: John 3v16

TABLE TALK

Recap what Jesus has told Nicodemus so far: What does everyone need to be? (*Born again*) Where did Jesus come from? (*Heaven*) What would happen to Jesus? (*He would be 'lifted up'.*)

Now Jesus is going to tell Nicodemus the most famous verse in the Bible. (But Nicodemus doesn't know that!)
Read John 3v16

READ

TALK

Who sent Jesus into the world? (*God*) Why did God send Jesus? (*Because He loved us, so that those who believe in Jesus may have eternal life.*)

DO

On the <u>back</u> of this page you will find the verse, but with some gaps in it. Fill in the gaps, then cut out the verse and put it somewhere you will all see it every day.

THINK

Family Challenge: This is the most famous verse in the Bible. Why not learn it! (*eg: you could sing it to a nursery rhyme—Old King Cole?—or maybe even rap it!*) Test each other every day for a week to check that you've really learnt it.

PRAY

God's everlasting love for us is the reason He sent Jesus. Thank God for loving you so much that He sent Jesus to die for you.

Building up
Together, think of one sentence to sum up why Jesus came.

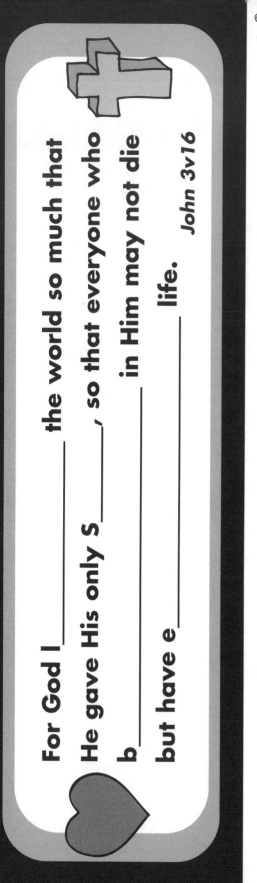

For God l _____ the world so much that

He gave His only S_____ , so that everyone who

b_____ in Him may not die _____

but have e_____ life.   *John 3v16*

Two ways to live

> ### KEYPOINT
> If we believe in Jesus, and come to Him to be forgiven, then we are found 'Not Guilty'.

Today's passages are:
Table Talk: John 3v17-21
XTB: John 3v17-21

TABLE TALK
Mime different ways of getting **light** (*eg: light a candle, pull cord on a bathroom light, switch on a torch...*) Ask the others to guess what you are miming.

READ
On Day 33 we saw that Jesus is like a **LIGHT** to people. He shows us the truth about ourselves. He helps us to see the sin in our lives. But some people don't want to be in the light...
Read John 3v17-21

TALK
In verse 19 what do people love and why? (v19) (*Darkness instead of light, because their deeds are evil.*) People run **away** from the light (away from Jesus) because they want to keep on sinning. They prefer to do what they want instead of what God wants.

DO
Jesus told Nicodemus that people like that are already condemned (judged). They are found **Guilty** and must be punished. **Draw a stick man.** *Write 'Guilty' under the picture.*

THINK
BUT we don't have to run away from God's light. We can run towards it instead. What happens if we believe in Jesus? (v18) (*We're not condemned.*) If we believe in Jesus, and come to Him to be forgiven, then we are found **Not Guilty** and won't be punished. *Write 'Not' before 'Guilty' on your picture.*

PRAY
Say sorry to God for the wrong things you've done this week. Thank Him for sending Jesus so you can be forgiven.

Building up
Have you learnt yesterday's memory verse yet? Try to say it while patting your head and rubbing your stomach!

DAY 49 A tale of three people

TABLE TALK

We've found out about two Johns in the last 18 days. Who are they? (*John the disciple who wrote the Gospel, and John the Baptist.*)

John A (the Disciple)
Why did John write his book? (*Check John 20v31 if you're not sure.*) John wrote about Jesus so that people may believe in Him and have eternal life.

John B (the Baptist)
What did John B do? (*Baptise people by dunking them under water as a sign that they want to be washed clean from sin.*)

But now Jesus has turned up, and <u>He</u> is baptising people too. Will John get jealous...? **Read John 3v22-30**

READ

Who did John say he <u>isn't</u>? (v28) (*The Christ/Messiah.*) What did he say about Jesus? (v30) (*'He must become greater; I must become less.'*) John says Jesus is like a bridegroom—the most important man at a wedding (v29). John is the bridegroom's friend who helps the bridegroom. John isn't jealous at all. In fact he's <u>happy</u> to serve Jesus!

TALK

John C (the unknown)
Actually there isn't a John C! The third person is **you**! John A <u>wrote</u> about Jesus. John B <u>spoke</u> about Jesus. How will **you** tell someone about Jesus this week? [*send a letter/email, invite them to church...*]

THINK

Choose a way, then ask God to help you.

PRAY

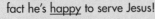

Building up
John B wanted **Jesus** to be seen as great, not himself. How can <u>you</u> be like that?

DAY 50
The one from above

TABLE TALK

We've reached the end of chapter three of John's book. The final verse sums up what we've learnt so far. It's about Jesus, 'the Son'. **Read John 3v36**

TALK

What will everyone who <u>believes</u> in Jesus have? (*Eternal life.*) What about those who reject (disobey) Jesus? (*They will not have eternal life.*) Believing in Jesus is the only way to be right with God and one day live with Him in heaven.

Do you remember looking at v36 before? (It was on Day 9.) It was summed up with this picture, showing that there are two ways to live.

THINK

Verse 36 is about a <u>choice</u>. Have you made that choice yet?

PRAY

• If you already believe in Jesus, and are following Him as King of your life, then thank Jesus for this. Ask Him to help you keep on living for Him every day.
• If you want to start following Jesus now, then turn back to Day 9. There is a prayer there that will help you.
• If you're not sure if you believe in Jesus (or if you want to) ask another Christian to talk to you about it. And ask God to help you understand and believe what the Bible says about Jesus.

Building up
The end of chapter three is all about **Jesus**, but doesn't use His name! He is called 'the one who comes from above'... **Read John 3v31-35**. What are we told about Jesus in v31? (*He comes from heaven and is greater than all.*) In v34? (*He is full of God's Spirit and speaks God's words.*) In v35? (*God loves His Son, Jesus, and has put everything in His power.*)

King David

Add some words or phrases to describe David.

CATCHING UP WITH DAVID

The book of 2 Samuel starts with the deaths of Saul and his son Jonathan.

David became the new king, just as God had promised. He captured Jerusalem and made it his royal city.

David brought the Ark of the Covenant to Jerusalem. It reminded the Israelites that **God was with them**.

KEYPOINT
David was God's chosen King, ruling over God's people in a way that was just and fair.

Today's passages are:
Table Talk: 2 Samuel 8v15
XTB: 2 Samuel 8v15

TABLE TALK

 DO

Today we're returning to the story of King David. Start by asking your children to think of some words or phrases to describe David and <u>write</u> them by his picture in **Notes for Parents**.
eg: trusted God, shepherd, beat Goliath, God's chosen king...

Read the rest of **Notes for Parents** to remind yourselves of the story so far from the book of 2 Samuel.

 READ

David was God's chosen king, ruling over God's people. **Read 2 Samuel 8v15** to see what kind of king he was.

What kind of king was David? (*He was just and fair.*)

 THINK

As we have read 1 and 2 Samuel, David has been a good example for us to follow. We've seen how he **trusts God** (eg: when fighting against Goliath); we've seen him show huge **kindness** to an enemy (eg: when he was kind to Jonathan's son Mephibosheth); and today we've been reminded that he was **just and fair**, doing what was <u>right</u> for his people.

 PRAY

Think carefully about your own lives. Are <u>you</u> like David? Do you want to be? Pray together about your answers.

Building up
David was a <u>good</u> king—but was he perfect? (*No!*) There's only one perfect King in the world. Who? (*Jesus*) What title reminds us that Jesus is our perfect King? (*'Christ'—this isn't Jesus' surname, it means 'God's chosen King'.*)

DAVID AND BATHSHEBA

Over the next few days we will be reading about David's adultery with Bathsheba, his attempts to cover it up and how God brings it out into the open.

This may raise some difficult issues for you or your children. It may be that you have experienced the pain of a marriage break-up. Certainly your children will know others who have. Reassure your child that God **loves** them, and each member of their family. Reassure them that you love them too. Encourage them to pray about any worries they have, and maybe to talk them through with an older Christian.

REASSURINGLY REAL

The Bible is real about people and life. We often have messy lives, where other people hurt us or we let ourselves down. The experiences of David, both in sinning and in receiving forgiveness, will help your child to be ready for the time when they mess up big time (which we all do!). They can learn, alongside David, that we have a God of grace who loves us, and who shows great mercy when we come to Him for forgiveness.

Sin is serious business—so serious that God sent His much loved Son to die because of it. We will treat it seriously in these pages. But we will also take the opportunity to rejoice at our wonderful, loving LORD, who knows our hearts, sees our sinfulness, and has provided a means of rescue for us. There's much to rejoice in!

KEYPOINT
David commited adultery with Bathsheba. He disobeyed God's laws.

Today's passages are:
Table Talk: 2 Samuel 11v1-4
XTB: 2 Samuel 11v1-4

TABLE TALK

Talk about times when you've seen what someone else has and wished it was yours
eg: their new car, mobile phone, bike, trainers…

READ

Today's story is a sad tale of King David seeing something that isn't his, but taking it anyway. **Read 2 Samuel 11v1-4**

TALK

What time of year was it? (v1) (*The time when kings go to war.*) But King David didn't go. Who did he send instead? (v1) (*Joab*) While Joab was leading the army, David was hanging around in his palace. One evening, while walking on the flat roof of his palace, he saw a beautiful woman. What was her name? (v3) (*Bathsheba*)

Bathsheba was married. One of God's laws says that you mustn't take someone else's wife or husband (Exodus 20v14). Did David keep God's law? (v4) (*No!*) When David saw Bathsheba, he wanted her. So he had her brought to the palace, where he slept with her. He disobeyed God.

THINK

When David saw Bathsheba he should have stopped looking straight away. Instead, he chose to find out more about her (v3). Then he gave in to temptation and took her. When you are tempted to do something wrong, walk away from it! Ask God to help you. He will!

PRAY

Building up
The Bible promises that God will always help us when tempted. Read this promise in **1 Corinthians 10v13**.

DAY 53
Trying to cover up

KEYPOINT
When David heard that Bathsheba was pregnant, he treid to cover up his sin.

Today's passages are:
Table Talk: 2 Samuel 11v5-13
XTB: 2 Samuel 11v5-13

TABLE TALK

<u>Recap:</u> What time of year was it? (*When kings go to war.*) Had David gone to war? (*No*) What did he see from the top of his palace? (*A beautiful woman.*) What did he do? (*Took her and slept with her.*)

READ

David had <u>disobeyed</u> God. Maybe he thought no-one would know what he'd done. But then he got a message from Bathsheba. **Read 2 Samuel 11v5**

TALK

What was her message? (v5) (*She was pregnant.*)

READ

Bathsheba was going to have a baby. But her husband Uriah was away with the army, so everyone would know that <u>he</u> couldn't be the father. So David came up with a sneaky plan. He'd bring Uriah back to give a report. Then Uriah would go home, sleep with his wife, and think <u>he'd</u> got her pregnant. But the plan didn't work! **Read 2 Samuel 11v6-13**

TALK

Where did David tell Uriah to go? (v8) (*Home*) Did Uriah go home? (v9) (*No*) Why not? (v11) (*Uriah believed it would be wrong to relax at home while the rest of the army were at war.*) David's rotten plan had failed. Tomorrow we'll see what he plans next...

PRAY

Two days ago we saw that David is often a good example for us to follow. But not this time!!! Are you ever tempted to cover things up when you've done something wrong? Ask God to help you to be honest and to own up when you're in the wrong.

Building up
Read verse 11 again. Compare what Uriah would <u>not</u> do with what David <u>had</u> done.

DAY 54
A horrible plan

KEYPOINT
David had Uriah killed in battle—but the LORD knew what he'd done, and was displeased.

Today's passages are:
Table Talk: 2 Samuel 11v14-17&26-27
XTB: 2 Samuel 11v14-27

TABLE TALK

Yesterday we read about David's rotten plan to make Uriah think he'd got Bathsheba pregnant. Why didn't David's plan work? (*Uriah refused to go home.*)

READ

But that didn't stop David! Now he planned something even worse...
Read 2 Samuel 11v14-17

TALK

What was David's plan this time? (v15) (*To have Uriah killed in battle.*)
Did this plan work? (v17) (*Yes*)

READ

David's horrid plan worked. Uriah was killed in battle. Now David could make Bathsheba his wife...
Read 2 Samuel 11v26-27

TALK

Bathsheba became David's wife, and later gave birth to her baby. Was it a boy or a girl? (v27) (*A boy*) It <u>looked</u> like David had got away with it. BUT how does v27 end? (*'The thing David had done displeased the LORD.'*) God knew <u>everything</u> that David had done. And He was **not** pleased! *Tomorrow we'll find out what God does about it...*

PRAY

<u>Nothing</u> we do is hidden from God! He knows everything about us. He knows all the good things we do and say and think. And He knows all the bad things too. How does that make you feel? Talk to God about it now.

Building up
Read 2 Samuel 11v18-25 to see how Joab became involved in David's cover up. Can you think of examples where your sin could end up involving others?

Notes for Parents

NATHAN'S STORY

"There were two men, one rich and the other poor"

"The rich man had loads of sheep and cows."

"The poor man had just one little lamb."

"The poor man loved his lamb like one of his own children."

"But then a traveller came to visit the rich man."

"The rich man could have killed one of his own sheep to feed his guest."

"But instead he killed and ate the poor man's lamb!"

Based on 2 Samuel 12v1-4.

Found out!

>
> **KEYPOINT**
> God sent Nathan to tell David a story. Like the rich man in the story, David deserved to die!

Today's passages are:
Table Talk: 2 Samuel 12v5-7a
XTB: 2 Samuel 12v1-7a

TABLE TALK

Recap: David had taken Uriah's husband and then had Uriah killed. Did God know what David had done? (*Yes*) How did God feel? (*Displeased*)

David sent a man called Nathan to see David. Nathan was a **prophet** (one of God's messengers). Nathan told David a story. Read his story in **Notes for Parents**.

READ

This was a clever story, as David was about to find out... **Read 2 Samuel 12v5-7a** (The 'a' means just read the <u>first</u> part of verse 7.)

TALK

How did David feel when he heard the story? (v5) (*Very angry*) What did he say the rich man deserved? (v5) (*He deserved to die.*) But what did Nathan tell David? (v7a) (*'You are the man!'*)

THINK

Which man was David like? (*The rich man.*) How? (*He had taken another man's wife, just like the rich man had taken another man's lamb.*)

David had been found out! He was just like the rich man in the story. And by his own lips he'd admitted that he deserved to die for what he'd done.

PRAY

David was right! The correct punishment for sin is death. That's why Jesus had to **die**, to take the punishment <u>we</u> deserve. More about that tomorrow, but for now spend some time **thanking Jesus** for taking that punishment in your place.

Building up
Read Nathan's story for yourselves in **v1-4**.

DAY 56
Amazing grace

KEYPOINT
God showed His grace to David by forgiving him, and rescuing him from the death penalty.

Today's passages are:
Table Talk: 2 Samuel 12v7-9 & 13
XTB: 2 Samuel 12v7-14

TABLE TALK

Read yesterday's picture story again.

Like the rich man in the story, David had taken something that wasn't his. What? (*Bathsheba, another man's wife.*) Let's see what God said about that...

READ

Read 2 Samuel 12v7-9

In verses 7 and 8 God reminds David of all the great things He has done for David. How many times does God say 'I' in these verses? (5—NIV, 4—Good News Bible) God had given David <u>so much!</u> He had no need to take another man's wife.

TALK

God would rightly punish David for disobeying Him (v10-12). Later on in 2 Samuel we'll see that coming true.

READ

Read David's response to God in **v13**.

What did David say? (v13) (*'I have sinned against the LORD.'*) David was right. He <u>had</u> sinned. The right punishment for his sin was death. But what did Nathan tell him? (v13) (*God had forgiven him, he wouldn't die.*)

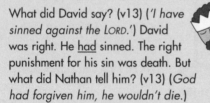

TALK

PRAY

Grace is God's huge kindness to people who don't deserve it. God showed His grace to David by forgiving him. How has God shown His grace to <u>you</u>? Talk about it, then thank God for His amazing grace.

Building up
David deserved to die for what he had done. But God forgave David, and rescued him from the death penalty. Does that remind you of anything? (*The way God forgives us because of Jesus.*) We all sin. The right punishment for sin is death. BUT, if we admit our sin (as David did), and put our trust in Jesus, then God will **forgive** us and **rescue** us from the punishment we deserve. Read this promise in **1 John 1v9**.

DAY 57
Facing consequences

KEYPOINT
David's newborn son died, as God said he would.

Today's passages are:
Table Talk: 2 Samuel 12v14-23
XTB: 2 Samuel 12v15-23

TABLE TALK

Note to Parents: David's newborn son dies in today's reading and this may worry your child. Reassure them with God's promise that EVERYTHING that happens to a Christian will be GOOD for them. (Romans 8v28)

READ

God forgave David for disobeying Him by stealing Uriah's wife. But David still had to face the consequences (results) of his sin. **Read 2 Samuel 12v14-17**

TALK

What did God say would happen to David's newborn baby? (v14) (*He would die.*) When the baby became ill, what did David do? (v16) (*He pleaded with God for the child, and he fasted—went without food.*)

READ

Read 2 Samuel 12v18-23

How did David react to his baby's death? (v20) (*He went to God's temple and worshipped.*)

THINK

While the baby was alive, David kept pleading with God. But now that the baby was dead, David <u>accepted</u> God's answer to his prayers. He didn't turn against God. David trusted God to carry out His perfect plans.

PRAY

God always answers our prayers. But sometimes the answer is 'No'. We may not understand why, but we can be sure that God is doing the right thing. Do you find that hard? Pray about it together.

Building up
Are you ever tempted to think that sin doesn't matter, because God will forgive you? It's true that God forgives sin, but we still have to live with the consequences of it (as David did). Sin <u>does</u> matter.

DAY 58
A son is born

KEYPOINT
God gave David a new son, called Solomon. God <u>loved</u> Solomon.

Today's passages are:
Table Talk: 2 Samuel 12v24-25
XTB: 2 Samuel 12v24-31

TABLE TALK

Talk about your names: Who chose them? Do you know what they mean? (eg: Paul means 'little', Sarah means 'princess' and Mark means 'large hammer'!!!)

READ

David and his wife Bathsheba had a new son. Read about his names in **2 Samuel 12v24-25**.

TALK

What did David call his son? (v24) (Solomon) What name did God give him? (v25) (Jedidiah) Look to see if your Bible has a note at the bottom of the page to tell you what this name means. ('Loved by the LORD') God <u>loved</u> Solomon. He would become the next king after David. He was the one who would build a temple for God.

THINK

God took David's sin (in taking Bathsheba from Uriah) and used it for His own good purposes (the birth of Solomon). Only God can bring good out of bad like that!

PRAY

Sometimes life is a mess. But God can bring good out of any situation, however awful. Thank Him for this, and ask Him to help you trust Him when things are tough.

Building up
All through the story of David and Bathsheba, the Israelites have been at war with the Ammonites. But now Joab, the leader of the Israelite army, is about to win it... **Read 2 Samuel 12v26-31**. Did David capture the enemy city of Rabbah? (v29) (Yes) David's victory was a sign that God had forgiven him. It was <u>God</u> who gave him victory.

DAY 59
Everlasting love

KEYPOINT
David knew he could ask God for mercy because of His fantastic love.

Today's passages are:
Table Talk: Psalm 51v1-2
XTB: Psalm 51v1-2

DO

Find a way of making a mark on each person's cheek eg: face paint, eye shadow, tomato ketchup... Leave it there while doing today's Table Talk.

READ

David had messed up—big time! But he didn't hide in his room, feeling terrible. He admitted his sin to God. And he wrote a psalm about it. (A psalm is a song or prayer to God.) We're going to read David's psalm in the next few days. **Read Psalm 51v1-2**

TALK

David uses a number of words in his psalm to write about his **sin**. Which does he use in your Bible? (eg: faults, sin, transgressions, iniquity, evil...) Sin is doing what <u>we</u> want instead of what <u>God</u> wants. What does David ask God to do with his sin? (v2) (Wash it away.)

Look at the marks on each others faces. They can be washed off. But you <u>can't</u> wash away the sin inside you! You can't clean up your own sin. But **God** can! He can wipe it away completely.

PRAY

Read verses 1 and 2 aloud as your own prayer to God. **Thank Him** for sending Jesus so that your sin can be washed away—and then wash your faces clean!

Building up
David knew he had sinned. But he also knew what <u>God</u> is like. How does David describe God's love? (v1) (Unfailing or constant.) God's everlasting love never runs out; never fails; never gives up. And because of God's fantastic love, David knows he can ask God for <u>mercy</u>. Look up mercy in a **dictionary**. Mercy is when God does <u>not</u> give us what we deserve. David deserved to be punished for his sin. But instead he asked His merciful God to forgive him. And God did!

DAY 60
Whiter than snow

KEYPOINT
David had sinned against God, and was sinful from birth. But God washed him whiter than snow.

Today's passages are:
Table Talk: Psalm 51v3-9
XTB: Psalm 51v3-9

TABLE TALK

I grew up in Scotland, and enjoyed sledging in deep snow most winters. What do _you_ like best about snow?

READ

David is still writing about his sin. **Read Psalm 51v3-9**

There's some tricky stuff in this psalm. Let's pick out two points:

1—David sinned against Uriah by taking his wife and then murdering him. But who does David say he has sinned against? (v4) (_God_) All sin is against **God**.

TALK

2—How long has David been sinful? (v5) (_Since he started to grow inside his mum_)

THINK

Do you know any babies? Even if they seem perfect now, they'll soon start proving how sinful they are! Sin isn't just doing wrong things. Sin is about what we're like _inside_, in our hearts. We all want to run our lives our own way, instead of letting God be our King.

How does David describe being forgiven? (v7) (_Whiter than snow._) The cool thing about snow is that it makes everything look white and clean. It's a great way to describe being forgiven. All David's sin had been washed away. He was **clean**.

PRAY

Imagine a l-o-n-g list of all your sin. Now imagine God washing it all away, leaving it whiter than snow. That's what it's like to be forgiven. How does that make you feel? Talk to God about it now.

Building up
Read v6 again. God <u>sees</u> everything. And He wants truth to run right through us. What does that mean for you this week? (_It's more than just not lying..._)

DAY 61
Heart disease

KEYPOINT
We are all born with spiritual heart disease. Only God can give us pure hearts.

Today's passages are:
Table Talk: Psalm 51v10-12
XTB: Psalm 51v10-12

TABLE TALK

Check each others pulse. (_Try putting two fingers lightly on your wrist, or the side of your neck._) The beat of your pulse shows that your heart is doing its job and working well. But some people have **heart disease**. Their heart doesn't work well, and they tire easily.

READ

Psalm 51 says that everyone is born with a kind of heart disease! Not <u>physical</u> heart disease, but <u>spiritual</u> heart disease. We are all born **sinful** (Psalm 51v5). Now read what David asks of God...
Read Psalm 51v10-12

TALK

What kind of heart does David ask for? (v10) (_A pure heart._)

THINK

If our <u>physical</u> hearts go wrong, we need an expert to give us heart surgery. The same is true for our <u>spiritual</u> hearts. We can't clean our hearts from sin. We can't fill them with God's Holy Spirit. But **God** can!

PRAY

Only **God** can give us pure hearts, to love and serve Him wholeheartedly. Read verses 10-12 again, aloud, as your own prayer to God.

Building up
On Day 45 we saw that Nicodemus should have recognised that Jesus' teaching about being 'born again' referred back to an Old T quote from Ezekiel. Read how God also promised a **new heart**, filled with His Holy Spirit, in **Ezekiel 36v25-27**.

DAY 62
Time to tell

KEYPOINT
David used his voice to tell sinners how to turn back to God, and to praise God.

Today's passages are:
Table Talk: Psalm 51v13-19
XTB: Psalm 51v13-19

TABLE TALK

(*You need pen & paper.*) Make a list or draw pics of different ways you use your <u>voice</u>. (*eg: shout, sing, whisper, pray...*)

READ

King David knew exactly what it was like to be sinful, so he was a great person to use his voice to tell other sinners about God... **Read Psalm 51v13-19**

TALK

What would David tell sinners? (v13) (*God's ways/commands.*) What would they do? (v13) (*Turn back to God.*) What else did David want to do with his voice? (v15) (*Praise God.*)

(*David also writes about <u>sacrifices</u>. Read **Building Up** below if you want to think more about that.*)

THINK

David longed to use his <u>voice</u> for God, to tell sinners how to **turn back** to God and be forgiven, and to **praise** God and tell others how wonderful He is. On your sheet of paper, list some ways that you can use <u>your</u> voices for God.

PRAY

Use your voices now to thank God that He's so wonderful, and ask Him to help you tell others about Him too.

Building up
Read v16-19 again. The Old T listed how and when to make **sacrifices** (gifts) to God. But David knew that God first looks at the **heart**—to see if people hate sin and love God. The only way to make a <u>right sacrifice</u> was by having a heart that's right with God.

DAY 63
Generation game

KEYPOINT
David knew God's greatness is so HUGE that it can't be measured!

Today's passages are:
Table Talk: Psalm 145v1-7
XTB: Psalm 145v1-7

TABLE TALK

Look up 'generation' in a dictionary. Talk about your family and friends, and work out who's the same generation as you, your parents, your grandparents...

READ

We're going to read another of David's psalms. This time he's falling over himself to tell us how wonderful God is! Listen out for words like **exalt**, **praise**, **extol** and **proclaim**. They all mean telling others (and God) how great God is.
Read Psalm 145v1-7

TALK

What does David call God? (v1) (*His God and King.*) David is a <u>king</u>, but he knows that **God** is the real King! How long is David going to praise God for? (v2) (*Always*) How great is God? (v3) (*His greatness is so HUGE it can't be measured/fathomed!!!*)

Who will speak about God's greatness? (v4) (*One generation will tell another.*) This means adults will tell children, grannies will tell grandchildren, uncles will tell nephews and so on...

PRAY

Think of someone from another generation who tells <u>you</u> about God. Thank God for this person. Ask Him to help them know the best way to tell you about God's greatness.

Building up
Find out how **Timothy**, one of Paul's helpers, was taught the Bible by his mother and grandmother: **read Acts 16v1, 2 Timothy 1v5** and **3v14-15.**

DAY 64
How good is that!

KEYPOINT
God is loving, merciful, good and always keeps His promises.

Today's passages are:
Table Talk : Psalm 145v8-16
XTB : Psalm 145v8-16

 TABLE TALK

David is bursting to tell us how good God is... **Read Psalm 145v8-16**

 DO

Copy v8-9 onto some paper, As you do, talk about what the verses mean. (eg: God is so _loving_ that He is _merciful_ [He doesn't treat us as we deserve]. Instead He is _gracious_ [showing huge kindness to us even though we don't deserve it].)

 TALK

Which verse says that God always keeps His promises? (_Verse 13_)

Do you have a favourite promise from the Bible? Talk about any favourites, and why you've chosen them.

 THINK

There are some very important truths in today's verses:
• God is loving
• God is merciful
• God is good
• God always keeps His promises.
Which one do you particularly want to remember today? Why did you choose that one?

 PRAY

Thank God for being so wonderful. Ask Him to help you get to know Him even better as you keep reading His book, the Bible.

Building up
Why not write in and tell me what your favourite promise is from the Bible, and why it's your favourite. I'll send you a **free** Promise Pencil. It has Psalm 145v13 written on it: 'The Lord is faithful to all His promises.'
 Write to: Table Talk, The Good Book Company, 37 Elm Road, New Malden, Surrey, KT3 3HB
or email me: alison@thegoodbook.co.uk

DAY 65
Near or far?

KEYPOINT
Our amazing, powerful God, who always does right, is <u>near</u> to us.

Today's passages are:
Table Talk : Psalm 145v17-21
XTB : Psalm 145v17-21

 TABLE TALK

David has been telling us how great God is. How great did David say He is? (_Too great to measure—v3_)

 READ

BUT have you ever thought that God is so great and powerful that He won't want to bother with you? If so, the last part of Psalm 145 is just what you need to hear...
Read Psalm 145v17-21

 TALK

What does David say God is like? (v17) (_Righteous_) Ask your child to try and work out what that means. (_When God is called righteous it means that He is always in the right, and does what is right._) Wow! God never thinks, does or says anything wrong!

What does David say in v18? (_God is near to all who call on Him._) Our amazing, powerful God—Who always does right—is **near** to us! He wants us to call on Him. He wants us to talk to Him (about every part of our lives, not just the BIG stuff.) How cool is that!

 THINK

Jot down some stuff you can talk to God about. Include things from your own life, your family, friends, school, work, and world news...

 PRAY

Our wonderful God will <u>always</u> listen to your prayers. He is **near** to you. Talk to Him now about some things on your list.

Building up
Some people like to wear a cross, or something like a WWJD bracelet (it stands for 'What would Jesus do?') to show that they are Christians. Can you think of anything you could do or wear that would remind you that **God is always near**?

Extra Readings

WHY ARE THERE EXTRA READINGS?

Table Talk and **XTB** both come out every three months. The main Bible reading pages contain material for 65 days. That's enough to use them Monday to Friday for three months.

Many families find that their routine is different at weekends from during the week. Some find that regular Bible reading fits in well on school days, but not at weekends. Others encourage their children to read the Bible for themselves during the week, then explore the Bible together as a family at weekends, when there's more time to do the activities together.

The important thing is to help your children get into the habit of reading the Bible for themselves—and that they see that regular

Bible reading is important for **you** as well.

If you **are** able to read the Bible with your children every day, that's great! The extra readings on the next page will augment the main **Table Talk** pages so that you have enough material to cover the full three months.

You could:

- Read **Table Talk** every day for 65 days, then use the extra readings for the rest of the third month.

- Read **Table Talk** on weekdays. Use the extra readings at weekends.

- Use any other combination that works for your family.

BEFORE DAVID WAS KING...

In this issue of Table Talk we've learnt about King David from the book of 2 Samuel. These 26 extra readings are like a flashback—to David's earlier life, before he was king...

King Saul quickly became jealous of David, and kept trying to kill him. But David knew that God

had promised to make him king, so he <u>trusted</u> God to save him. And God did!

There are 26 Bible readings on the next three pages. Part of each verse has been printed for you—but with a word missing. Fill in the missing words as you read the verses. Then see if you can find them all in the wordsearch.

Note: Some are written backwards—or diagonally!!

S	P	I	R	I	T	U	J	O	N	A	T	H	A	N
O	H	A	S	E	E	N	E	T	W	L	V	X	T	B
K	I	N	G	D	O	M	S	F	A	M	I	L	Y	D
B	L	U	E	R	A	E	P	S	N	A	C	K	G	E
W	I	N	D	O	W	H	I	S	T	A	T	I	O	N
E	S	C	L	U	C	K	N	A	L	P	O	S	A	I
L	T	W	O	H	U	N	D	R	E	D	R	I	T	M
L	I	A	R	O	T	H	U	R	R	Y	Y	D	S	R
E	N	A	D	A	V	I	D	O	E	S	H	E	L	E
M	E	A	F	R	A	I	D	W	B	I	B	L	E	T
A	S	R	E	H	T	A	F	S	O	F	A	B	L	E
N	J	E	A	L	O	U	S	X	R	W	O	R	L	D

Extra Readings

1 ☐ **Read 1 Samuel 17v45**
Flashback 1: Goliath challenged the Israelite army to fight him—but they were all too scared! But David knew that <u>God</u> was on his side...
"You come against me with sword and spear and javelin, but I come against you in the
n _ _ _ of the Lord Almighty." (v45)

2 ☐ **Read 1 Samuel 17v46-49**
Flashback 2: David knew that God would give him victory over Goliath. He was right!
"The whole **W** _ _ _ _ will know that there is a God in Israel." (v46)

3 ☐ **Read 1 Samuel 18v1-4**
David was now living at King's Saul's palace. He became good friends with Saul's son, Jonathan.
'**J** _ _ _ _ _ _ _ _ made a covenant (binding agreement) with David because he loved him as himself.' (v3)

4 ☐ **Read 1 Samuel 18v5-9**
Everything David did was a success. But that made Saul jealous of David!
'From that time on Saul kept a
J _ _ _ _ _ _ eye on David.' (v9)

5 ☐ **Read 1 Samuel 18v10-11**
Ever since Saul had turned away from God, he had been bothered by an evil spirit. David's harp playing helped Saul, but one day Saul attacked David!
'Saul threw the spear, saying to himself, "I'll pin David to the **W** _ _ _ ." But David dodged him twice.' (v11)

6 ☐ **Read 1 Samuel 18v12-16**
Everything David did was a success, because God was with him.
'In everything he did he had great success because the **L** _ _ _ was with him.' (v14)

7 ☐ **Read 1 Samuel 18v17-19**
Saul told David he could marry Saul's daughter, Merab, as long as David fought in battles. Saul hoped David would die fighting the Philistines!
'Saul said to himself, "I will not raise a hand against David. Let the
P _ _ _ _ _ _ _ _ _ _ do that!"' (v17)

8 ☐ **Read 1 Samuel 18v20-25**
Saul offered his second daughter, Michal, to David for the price of 100 Philistine foreskins (skin at the end of the penis). Saul hoped those Philistines would kill David!
'Saul's **p** _ _ _ was to have David killed by the Philistines.' (v25)

9 ☐ **Read 1 Samuel 18v26-30**
David killed <u>twice</u> as many Philistines as needed, without being hurt! Saul's wicked plan had failed!
'David and his men went out and killed
t _ _ **h** _ _ _ _ _ _ Philistines.' (v27)

10 ☐ **Read 1 Samuel 19v1-3**
Saul told Jonathan that he wanted to kill David. But Jonathan warned David about his father's plans.
'Jonathan warned David,
"My **f** _ _ _ _ _ is looking for a chance to kill you."' (v2)

Extra Readings

11 ☐ **Read 1 Samuel 19v4-7**

Jonathan reminded Saul that David had risked his own life to save the Israelites from Goliath. So Saul promised not to kill David. "The Lord won a great

v _ _ _ _ _ _ for Israel.
When you saw it, you were glad." (v5)

12 ☐ **Read 1 Samuel 19v8-12**

Although he'd promised not to, Saul again tried to kill David with his spear. Then Saul sent men to David's house to kill him. 'Michal let David down from a

w _ _ _ _ _ _ ',
and he ran away
and escaped.' (v12)

13 ☐ **Read 1 Samuel 19v13-17**

Michal helped David escape. Then she put a statue (idol) into David's bed, and pretended it was David!
'Michal took an idol and laid it on the bed, covering it with a garment and putting some

g _ _ _ _ ' _ hair at the head.' (v13)

14 ☐ **Read 1 Samuel 19v18-24**

David escaped and joined Samuel. Every time Saul's men came near David, they started prophesying (singing praise to God). When Saul himself went to catch David, he started to prophesy too!
'But the **S** _ _ _ _ _ _ of God even came upon Saul, and he walked along prophesying all the way to Naioth.' (v23)

15 ☐ **Read 1 Samuel 20v1-4**

Jonathan agreed to do anything David wanted, to save him from Saul.
'Jonathan said to David, "Whatever you **w** _ _ _ me to do, I'll do for you."' (v4)

16 ☐ **Read 1 Samuel 20v5-13**

David and Jonathan made a plan. David wouldn't come to the feast at Saul's table. Jonathan would then tell David if Saul was angry or not.
'David said, "If Saul says, 'All right,' I will be safe; but if he becomes angry, you will know that he is

d _ _ _ _ _ _ _ _ _
to harm me."' (v7)

17 ☐ **Read 1 Samuel 20v14-17**

Jonathan asked David to show kindness to his family. David kept this promise many years later. (2 Samuel 9)
'Jonathan said, "Do not ever cut off your kindness from my **f** _ _ _ _ _ ."' (v15)

18 ☐ **Read 1 Samuel 20v18-23**

Jonathan said that he would use arrows as a secret sign to tell David about Saul's plans.
"I will shoot three **a** _ _ _ _ _ at it, as though it were a target." (v20)

19 ☐ **Read 1 Samuel 20v24-33**

When Saul saw that David hadn't come to the feast, he was furious. He even tried to kill his son Jonathan!
'Saul threw his **S** _ _ _ _ _ at Jonathan to kill him, and Jonathan realised that his father was really determined to kill David.' (v33)

20 ☐ **Read 1 Samuel 20v34-42**

Jonathan used some arrows to warn David about Saul, as they'd agreed. Jonathan shouted to the boy with him, but the message was really for David.
'Jonathan shouted, "**H** _ _ _ _ _ ! Go quickly! Don't stop!"' (v38)

Extra Readings

21 ☐ **Read 1 Samuel 23v14-18**

We're skipping ahead a few chapters to see how Jonathan helps David again. This time Jonathan reminds David to trust in God's promise that David will be the next king.
'Jonathan said, "Don't be **a** _ _ _ _ _ . My father Saul won't be able to harm you. You will be king over Israel."' (v17)

22 ☐ **Read 1 Samuel 23v19-23**

Some people from a town called Ziph agreed to help Saul catch David.
'Saul said, "Find out for certain where David is, and who has **s** _ _ _ him there."' (v22)

23 ☐ **Read 1 Samuel 23v24-29**

Saul was chasing David round a hill, when a messenger arrived to tell Saul he had to come back and fight the Philistines. God had saved David!
'Saul and his men were on one **s** _ _ _ of the hill, and David and his men were on the other side, hurrying to get away from Saul.' (v26)

WHAT NEXT?

We hope that **Table Talk** has helped you get into a regular habit of reading the Bible with your children.

Table Talk comes out every three months. Each issue contains 65 full **Table Talk** outlines, plus 26 days of extra readings. By the time you've used them all, the next issue will be available.

Available from your local Christian bookshop—or call us on **0845 225 0880** to order a copy.

24 ☐ **Read 1 Samuel 24v1-7**

Saul went into a cave to go to the toilet. It was the cave David and his men were hiding in! David crept up and cut Saul's robe.
'David crept up unnoticed and cut off a corner of Saul's **r** _ _ _ .' (v4)

25 ☐ **Read 1 Samuel 24v8-15**

David showed Saul the cut off corner from his robe—as proof that David wasn't trying to kill Saul.
'David shouted, "Look at the piece of your robe I am holding. I could have killed you, but instead I only **c** _ _ this off."' (v11)

26 ☐ **Read 1 Samuel 24v16-22**

Saul says David will be king of Israel one day. As we know from the book of 2 Samuel, Saul is right!
'Saul said, "I know that you will surely be king, and that the **k** _ _ _ _ _ _ of Israel will continue under your rule."' (v20)

COMING SOON!
Issue Ten of Table Talk

Issue Ten of Table Talk explores the books of John and 1 and 2 Kings.

- The Gospel of **John** tells us all about Jesus. Read about some more of the miracles that pointed to <u>who</u> Jesus is.
- Find out more about David's son Solomon, and the kings who came after him, in the books of **1 and 2 Kings**.